THE
FREEDOM
JOURNAL
ACCOMPLISH YOUR #1 GOAL IN 100 DAYS

TheFreedomJournal.com

THREE REASONS YOU'LL LOVE

THE
FREEDOM
JOURNAL

1. Success. The #1 reason people are successful? They know how to set and accomplish goals. With The Freedom Journal, you have the framework to do the same.

2. F.O.C.U.S. **F**ollow **O**ne **C**ourse **U**ntil **S**uccess. Loss of focus results in failure. The Freedom Journal provides laser focus all the way to the accomplishment of your #1 goal!

3. Accountability. Lack of accountability is why you've failed in the past. The Freedom Journal is an accountability partner that WON'T let you fail!

ISBN: 978-0-9962340-1-6

Printed in China

Designed by Sutton Long

Illustration placement by Brandy Shea

Edited by Whitney Henry

Logistics by Richie Norton of Prouduct.com

SECOND EDITION

THE
FREEDOM
JOURNAL

ACCOMPLISH YOUR #1 GOAL IN 100 DAYS

Because we all need a little help
accomplishing our goals...

DEDICATION

The Freedom Journal is dedicated to the listeners of EOFire.
Fire Nation, you've shown me what's possible when BIG goals are set
and accomplished. You've been my accountability partner
on this journey, and for that I salute you!

EOFire.com

FREQUENTLY ASKED QUESTIONS

What happens if I miss a day?

First things first: learn something from it! Why did you miss a day, and how can you prevent missing days in the future? Next: pick right back up where you left off and keep working towards your #1 goal!

What if I have more than one goal?

Awesome! Be sure to subscribe at TheFreedomJournal.com and you'll receive a discounted Freedom Journal every 100 days!

Is there a place I can go to meet others who may be working towards a similar goal?

Yes! Join us in our private Facebook group, which is filled with thousands of Freedom Lovers who are also accomplishing their #1 goal in 100 days. EOFire.com/facebook.

How do I snag my digital files?

Visit EOFire.com/digital. Enter password "1216" for access.

Is there a place where all the resources are listed out?

Yes! All of the resources are listed out starting on page 303 of your Freedom Journal.

What are the different color bookmarks for?

GOLD: The current day you are on.
ORANGE: Details of the 10-day sprint you are currently completing.
BLACK: Your choice! The calendar? The last quarterly review you completed? The Table of Contents?

Are you ready to master
productivity, discipline, and focus in 100 days?

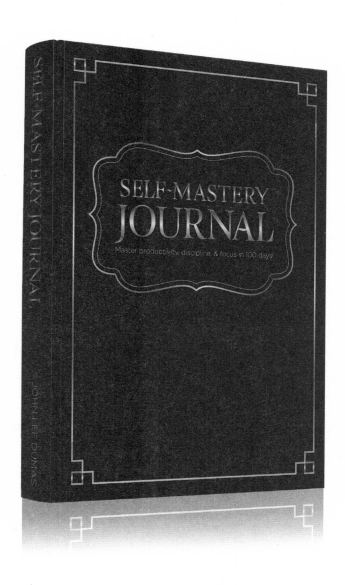

Then it's time for:

SELF~MASTERY

JOURNAL

Master productivity, discipline, & focus in 100 days!

By John Lee Dumas

THE resource that will guide you in mastering your productivity, discipline, and focus in 100 days.

Learn more at:

SelfMasteryJournal.com

TABLE OF CONTENTS

WHAT'S IN MY JOURNAL

GETTiNG STARTED
—USING MY JOURNAL—

START

THE FREEDOM JOURNAL

Goals.

We all have them, but why is accomplishing them such a challenge?

In one word: accountability.

We live in a fast-paced, busy, loud world. It's easy to see why things get put off 'til tomorrow way too often.

With The Freedom Journal, that all changes.

The Freedom Journal is what YOU need to accomplish your #1 goal in 100 days.

We've tried holding ourselves accountable, and that failed. Guess what? We're human.

We've tried having others hold us accountable, and that also failed. Guess what? They're human, too.

The Freedom Journal is not human. It's a POWERFUL weapon that, when wielded correctly, can produce amazing results in a short time.

If you can commit to The Freedom Journal and follow the framework, then you will accomplish your goal. Period.

The Freedom Journal is engineered to provide you with the direction and accountability to accomplish your #1 goal—a goal that has been elusive for far too long.

What is a goal you want to accomplish in 100 days?

Say it out loud.

Imagine how it would FEEL to have accomplished this goal.

Pretty awesome, right?!

You can do this. With The Freedom Journal by your side encouraging you every step of the way, you WILL accomplish your goal, and it will be amazing.

Let's get started!

WHAT IS THE FREEDOM JOURNAL?

The Freedom Journal is your guide to accomplishing your #1 goal in 100 days.

HOW THE FREEDOM JOURNAL WORKS

The Freedom Journal is 100 days of accountability.

Step-by-step, The Freedom Journal will guide you towards your goal.

THE THREE STEPS TO SUCCESS

Step 1: Establish a "S.M.A.R.T." goal (details on the next page).
Step 2: Take daily action with guidance from The Freedom Journal.
Step 3: Accomplish your goal!

SPRINTS AND REVIEWS

10-day sprints: To ensure you stay true to your timeline, there will be 10-day sprints where you will accomplish micro-goals.

Quarterly review: Every 25 days, you'll review your progress to identify what's been working and where you are struggling. Then you'll amplify the success and correct the areas of weakness.

K.I.S.S.
KEEP IT SUPER SIMPLE

Many people try to complicate the simplest things.

Do not complicate The Freedom Journal.

Simply wake up every day, follow the guidance, and execute.

You are 100 days away from accomplishing your goal.

Let's do this!

HOW TO ESTABLISH A "S.M.A.R.T." GOAL

S - Specific
M - Measurable
A - Attainable
R - Relevant
T - Time-bound

Definiteness of purpose is the starting point of all achievement. —W. CLEMENT STONE

Specific: Your goal MUST be clear.

What: What do I want to accomplish?
Why: Specific reasons, purpose, or benefits of accomplishing the goal.
Who: Who is involved?
Where: Identify a location.
Which: Identify requirements and constraints.

Success is the sum of small efforts, repeated day in and day out. —ROBERT COLLIER

Measurable: You MUST be able to track your progress, and measure the level of success. Your goal needs to answer questions such as:

How much?
How many?
How will I know when it is accomplished?

Perfection is not attainable, but if we chase perfection we can catch excellence. —VINCE LOMBARDI

Attainable: "Building the next Google" is not an attainable goal in the next 100 days. "Launching a podcast by following the free tutorials at FreePodcastCourse.com" is.

You must set an attainable goal: a goal you can realistically accomplish in the given time frame.

> ## Our greatest fear should not be of failure but of succeeding at things in life that don't really matter.
> —FRANCIS CHAN

Relevant: Your goal has to matter in relation to your overall life. You don't want to get to the end of this journey, accomplish your goal, and say, "That was good, but this accomplishment hasn't impacted my life in a major way."

We want IMPACT!

A relevant goal should answer yes to these questions:

• Does this seem worthwhile?

• Will the impact positively affect me, and those around me?

• Is this the right time to pursue this specific goal?

> PARKINSON'S LAW: ## Work expands so as to fill the time available for its completion.

Time-bound: This is where The Freedom Journal THRIVES. You must set your goal within a time frame. This will prevent your goal from being overtaken by the day-to-day crises that happen to us all.

If you DON'T put time constraints on your goal, the time to accomplish it will expand indefinitely.

You'll be establishing your own S.M.A.R.T. goal in just a few pages, but first...

ARE YOU READY?

The next 100 days are going to come and go before you know it. How many more months will slip by without any major accomplishment? Are you ready to put your foot down, dig your heel in, and COMMIT to accomplishing an amazing goal?

> ## I have learned over the years that when one's mind is made up, this diminishes fear. —ROSA PARKS

Accountability partner

The Freedom Journal is your accountability partner on this journey. A great way to add to this is to have a real-life accountability partner to go on this journey with.

If you and a friend both commit to an individual 100-day goal and check in with each other every few days, your chances of success increase greatly.

Whether you are going at it with a friend or alone, you have in your hands the most important tool you need.

Commit. Engage. Persevere.

The Freedom Journal team is rooting you on. It's time to IGNITE!

Visit EOFire.com/facebook to join The Freedom Journal private Facebook group, where you can connect with like-minded people and engage with the thousands of other Freedom Lovers who are on the same path as you!

SAMPLE S.M.A.R.T. GOAL

Goal: I want to publish my first book in 100 days!

Specific

What: I want to self-publish a book on the top 10 ways to get a better night's sleep in 100 days in the Amazon bookstore.
Why: Because I have the knowledge and I know it will help thousands of people if I can get it down on paper and into a distribution center like Amazon.
Who: Me, my editor, my formatter, and my designer.
Where: I will do all the work from my living room computer.
Which: (Constraints) I must finish the book by day 60 to give my editor and designer time to do their magic!

Measurable

The book will be approximately 250 pages, so I will write 5 pages a day for the first 50 days, and use the last 10 days to self-edit and finalize. While my editor and designer are working on the book in the final 40 days, I will turn my efforts to pre-marketing.

I will use the 10-day sprints and quarterly reviews to ensure I stay on pace and on mission.

Attainable

I can write 5 pages a day! What makes me think this is possible? The Freedom Journal, that's what!

Relevant

Absolutely! I want to be an author as well as an authority figure in the sleep niche. This will help me achieve both!

Time-bound

This part defines The Freedom Journal. I am grateful to have its companionship along my journey, and can't wait to get started. From blank Word doc to published author and authority figure in 100 days, here I come!

P.S.: The above goal is fictional, but I recommend *Sleep Smarter* by Shawn Stevenson if you're intrigued by the title.

MY S.M.A.R.T. GOAL
It's time to set YOUR goal!

In 100 days I will: _____

_____

_____

Specific

_____

_____

_____

Measurable

_____

_____

_____

Attainable

_____

_____

_____

Relevant

_____

_____

_____

Time-bound

_____

_____

_____

SAMPLE ENTRIES

SAMPLE FIRST SPRINT

The micro-goal I will accomplish during this sprint:

I will write the first 50 pages of my book!

Three specific actions I will take to accomplish this micro-goal:

1. I will write a minimum of 5 pages a day

2. I will schedule three interviews with top sleep experts in the industry

3. I will exercise in some capacity daily!

One habit I will implement over the next 10 days:

I will get into a rhythm where I'm getting 7-8 hours of quality sleep every night!

My action plan to implement this habit:

I will be in bed by 9:30pm every night, with the goal of awaking at 5:30am to start my morning ritual!

It's time to IGNITE!

SAMPLE DAY

Try not to become a person of success,
but rather try to become a person of value. —ALBERT EINSTEIN

I am grateful for:
I am grateful for the opportunity to accomplish my dream goal. Now it's up to me to take action! I am grateful to have a project I am excited about that I know will help thousands of people get a better night's sleep!

In 99 days I will: (This is where you restate your goal EVERY day.)
Self-publish my book, Top 10 Ways to Get a Better Night's Sleep.

My #1 focus today is: write the first 5 pages of my book. So exciting!

By the end of the day I will have accomplished these three measurable objectives that support my S.M.A.R.T. goal:

1. Written 5 pages.

2. Locked in one authority figure on sleeping to interview.

3. Have a tidy work environment.

Action plan for the day:

O Meditate for 20 minutes.

O Write 5 pages.

O Contact ten sleep authority figures to lock in one for an interview.

O Clean up my work space so it feels like an environment conducive to work.

O For 53 minutes I will have no distractions and will simply write. After 53 minutes of distraction-free writing, I'll take a 7-minute break. Then I will take 20 minutes to review what I've written.

Thoughts/ideas/musings:
I thought writing a book was going to be a scary and daunting proposition, but when I break it down in this manner it truly seems doable...almost easy. I am very knowledgeable on sleep and can easily write 5 pages a day, if I simply sit down and write. OK, gotta go...it's writing time!

Recommended Resource: Hootsuite: Enhance your social media management with Hootsuite, the leading social media dashboard.

SAMPLE NIGHT

Two wonderful things that happened today:

1. I finished my first 5 pages of my book! I can do this!

2. While I was writing I had two AHA moments that came from my writing. I am shocked I never thought of these ideas before, but I can't wait to incorporate them into the book. Will share soon!

Two struggles I encountered:

1. A couple of times I didn't take the full 7-minute break as I was on a roll, but I hit a wall and my writing suffered. I need to stick to my plan.

2. 20 minutes is not long enough to review my 53 minutes of writing. I kept running out of time.

Possible solutions for these struggles:

1. Commit to the plan, John. You can do this!

2. I will bump my review time to 30 minutes starting tomorrow.

Tomorrow will be a great day because:
I have CONFIDENCE that I can and will finish this book. Today was not terrifying or exhausting, it was thrilling and energizing! I can't wait to wake up fresh and ready to tackle the next 5 pages of my book!

Final thought of the day:
Life is about the journey, not the destination. I have to make sure to enjoy this journey to my goal, each and every day, for what it is.

 Goodnight, Fire Nation!

SAMPLE 10-DAY SPRINT RECAP

My major accomplishment during this sprint:

I was actually able to sit down and write 5 pages EVERY day. There were many days I didn't want to, but I had made the commitment to myself and to The Freedom Journal.

My two biggest struggles during this sprint:

1. Getting to bed by 9:30pm every night.

2. Avoiding distractions that sabotage my 5-page daily commitment.

Two possible solutions to these struggles:

1. Go screen-free at 8:30pm every night to begin the evening wind down.

2. Use the SelfControl app to block Facebook (my biggest nemesis) from 8am to 2pm daily.

Two accomplishments I am most proud of:

1. 50 COMPLETED pages in my book!

2. I feel (and look) great thanks to my daily exercise!

I want to put a ding in the universe. —STEVE JOBS

Thoughts/ideas/musings:

I seriously can't believe that in 10 days I already have 50 pages written! It has taken me 5 years to start this dream goal, and now by committing to just 5 pages a day I am 10% of the way to my goal of a published book!

Fill in your current progress to your 100-day goal!　　　　⌐ BONUS ⌐

　　　25%　　　　50%　　　　75%　　　100%　　　125%

CONGRATULATIONS!
YOU'VE COMPLETED 10% OF YOUR 100 DAYS!

SAMPLE QUARTERLY REVIEW

Big accomplishments in the last 25 days:

1. I have 125 COMPLETED pages in my book...halfway to completion...YAY!

2. I have been tracking my own sleep and testing different strategies to prove and disprove different hypotheses. This is fun!

3. I have been doing a daily 35-minute power walk to start the day...yay!

Areas I need to improve in the next 25 days:

1. I had wanted to interview six sleep experts in these 25 days and I interviewed only two. I need a lot more time to reach out and schedule these chats.

2. I had wanted to start learning how to do a podcast to help market my book when it's live. I will have to sign up at FreePodcastCourse.com today to get going on that!

3. Cutting out distractions. I will keep using the SelfControl app to block my use of social media and stay on task!

I am proud that:
I stuck to my goal of 5 pages a day!

I am excited about:
The next 25 days. I will be talking about my completed book at that time!

I am surprised by:
The ease and power of doing the small things right every day, and how that adds up to something substantial in a relatively short period of time!

Thoughts/ideas/musings:
Once you start working on a project with consistency, it's unbelievable the ideas that start springing to mind. Just by constantly working my idea muscle in the daily writing of this book, I have had breakthroughs in mere days that have previously taken years! I can't wait to see what the next 75 days unveil!

CONGRATULATIONS!
YOU'VE COMPLETED 25% OF YOUR 100 DAYS!

MY S.M.A.R.T. GOAL
that I WILL accomplish in 100 days:

_____
_____
_____
_____
_____
_____
_____

YOUR JOURNEY BEGINS NOW

ON YOUR MARK

—10-DAY SPRINT—

FIRST 10-DAY SPRINT

The micro-goal I will accomplish during this sprint:

_____

_____

_____

Three specific actions I will take to accomplish this micro-goal:

1.

2.

3.

One habit I will implement over the next 10 days:

My action plan to implement this habit:

_____

_____

_____

DAY 1   Date:

If you really want to do something, you'll find a way.
If you don't, you'll find an excuse. —JIM ROHN

I am grateful for:

In 99 days I will (state your goal):

My #1 focus today is:

By the end of the day I will have accomplished these three measurable objectives that support my S.M.A.R.T. goal.

1.

2.

3.

Action plan for the day:

O

O

O

O

O

Thoughts/ideas/musings:

_____

_____

_____

_____

Recommended Resource: Hootsuite: Enhance your social media management with Hootsuite, the leading social media dashboard.

NIGHT 1

Two wonderful things that happened today:

1.

2.

Two struggles I encountered:

1.

2.

Possible solutions for these struggles:

1.

2.

Tomorrow will be a great day because:

_____
_____
_____
_____
_____

Final thought of the day:

_____
_____
_____
_____
_____

 Goodnight, Fire Nation!

DAY 2   Date:

Courage is resistance to fear, mastery of fear— not absence of fear. —MARK TWAIN

I am grateful for:

In 98 days I will (state your goal):

My #1 focus today is:

By the end of the day I will have accomplished these three measurable objectives that support my S.M.A.R.T. goal.

1.

2.

3.

Action plan for the day:

O

O

O

O

O

Thoughts/ideas/musings:

_____

_____

_____

_____

Recommended Resource: WorkFlowy: An organizational tool that makes life easier. It's a surprisingly powerful way to take notes, make lists, collaborate, brainstorm, and plan.

NIGHT 2

Two wonderful things that happened today:

1.

2.

Two struggles I encountered:

1.

2.

Possible solutions for these struggles:

1.

2.

Tomorrow will be a great day because:

_____

_____

_____

_____

_____

Final thought of the day:

_____

_____

_____

_____

_____

 Goodnight, Fire Nation!

DAY 3 Date:

Motivation is what gets you started.
Habit is what keeps you going. —JIM RYUN

I am grateful for:

In 97 days I will (state your goal):

My #1 focus today is:

By the end of the day I will have accomplished these three measurable objectives that support my S.M.A.R.T. goal.

1.

2.

3.

Action plan for the day:

-
-
-
-
-

Thoughts/ideas/musings:

_____

_____

_____

_____

Recommended Resource: Buffer: Makes it easy to share any page you're reading. Keep your Buffer topped up and they automatically share posts for you throughout the day.

NIGHT 3

Two wonderful things that happened today:

1.

2.

Two struggles I encountered:

1.

2.

Possible solutions for these struggles:

1.

2.

Tomorrow will be a great day because:

_____
_____
_____
_____
_____

Final thought of the day:

_____
_____
_____
_____
_____

 Goodnight, Fire Nation!

DAY 4   Date:

The starting point of all achievement is desire.

—NAPOLEON HILL

I am grateful for:

In 96 days I will (state your goal):

My #1 focus today is:

By the end of the day I will have accomplished these three measurable objectives that support my S.M.A.R.T. goal.

1.

2.

3.

Action plan for the day:

O

O

O

O

O

Thoughts/ideas/musings:

_____

_____

_____

_____

Recommended Resource: FourHourWorkWeek.com: #1 *New York Times* best-selling author Tim Ferriss teaches you how to escape the 9-5, live anywhere, and join the new rich.

NIGHT 4

Two wonderful things that happened today:

1.

2.

Two struggles I encountered:

1.

2.

Possible solutions for these struggles:

1.

2.

Tomorrow will be a great day because:

_____

_____

_____

_____

_____

Final thought of the day:

_____

_____

_____

_____

_____

 Goodnight, Fire Nation!

DAY 5   Date:

People often say that motivation doesn't last. Well, neither does bathing—that's why we recommend it daily. —ZIG ZIGLAR

I am grateful for:

In 95 days I will (state your goal):

My #1 focus today is:

By the end of the day I will have accomplished these three measurable objectives that support my S.M.A.R.T. goal.

1.

2.

3.

Action plan for the day:

O

O

O

O

O

Thoughts/ideas/musings:

_____

_____

_____

_____

Recommended Resource: Lynda: Learn software, creative, and business skills to achieve your personal and professional goals.

NIGHT 5

Two wonderful things that happened today:

1.

2.

Two struggles I encountered:

1.

2.

Possible solutions for these struggles:

1.

2.

Tomorrow will be a great day because:

_____

_____

_____

_____

_____

Final thought of the day:

_____

_____

_____

_____

_____

 Goodnight, Fire Nation!

DAY 6   Date:

Don't be afraid to give up the good to go for the great.

—JOHN D. ROCKEFELLER

I am grateful for:

In 94 days I will:

My #1 focus today is:

By the end of the day I will have accomplished these three measurable objectives that support my S.M.A.R.T. goal.

1.

2.

3.

Action plan for the day:

○

○

○

○

○

Thoughts/ideas/musings:

_____

_____

_____

_____

Recommended Resource: Fiverr: The place for people to share things they're willing to do for $5.

41

NIGHT 6

Two wonderful things that happened today:

1.

2.

Two struggles I encountered:

1.

2.

Possible solutions for these struggles:

1.

2.

Tomorrow will be a great day because:

_____

_____

_____

_____

_____

Final thought of the day:

_____

_____

_____

_____

_____

 Goodnight, Fire Nation!

DAY 7   Date:

There are two types of people who will tell you that you cannot make a difference in this world: those who are afraid to try and those who are afraid you will succeed. —RAY GOFORTH

I am grateful for:

In 93 days I will:

My #1 focus today is:

By the end of the day I will have accomplished these three measurable objectives that support my S.M.A.R.T. goal.

1.

2.

3.

Action plan for the day:

O

O

O

O

O

Thoughts/ideas/musings:

_____
_____
_____
_____

Recommended Resource: Evernote: The Evernote family of products help you remember and act upon ideas, projects and experiences across all the computers, phones and tablets you use.

NIGHT 7

Two wonderful things that happened today:

1.

2.

Two struggles I encountered:

1.

2.

Possible solutions for these struggles:

1.

2.

Tomorrow will be a great day because:

_____

_____

_____

_____

_____

Final thought of the day:

_____

_____

_____

_____

_____

 Goodnight, Fire Nation!

DAY 8   Date:

The whole secret of a successful life is to find out what is one's destiny to do, and then do it. —HENRY FORD

I am grateful for:

In 92 days I will:

My #1 focus today is:

By the end of the day I will have accomplished these three measurable objectives that support my S.M.A.R.T. goal.

1.

2.

3.

Action plan for the day:

O

O

O

O

O

Thoughts/ideas/musings:

_____

_____

_____

_____

Recommended Resource: EOFire.com: In his award-winning podcast, John Lee Dumas chats with today's most inspiring entrepreneurs 7 days a week. Prepare to IGNITE!

NIGHT 8

Two wonderful things that happened today:

1.

2.

Two struggles I encountered:

1.

2.

Possible solutions for these struggles:

1.

2.

Tomorrow will be a great day because:

_____

_____

_____

_____

_____

Final thought of the day:

_____

_____

_____

_____

_____

 Goodnight, Fire Nation!

DAY 9 Date:

If you are not willing to risk the unusual, you will have to settle for the ordinary. —JIM ROHN

I am grateful for:

In 91 days I will:

My #1 focus today is:

By the end of the day I will have accomplished these three measurable objectives that support my S.M.A.R.T. goal.

1.

2.

3.

Action plan for the day:

O

O

O

O

O

Thoughts/ideas/musings:

_____

_____

_____

_____

Recommended Resource: Jing: Try Jing for a free and simple way to start sharing images and short videos of your computer screen. For work, home, or play.

NIGHT 9

Two wonderful things that happened today:

1.

2.

Two struggles I encountered:

1.

2.

Possible solutions for these struggles:

1.

2.

Tomorrow will be a great day because:

_____
_____
_____
_____
_____

Final thought of the day:

_____
_____
_____
_____
_____

 Goodnight, Fire Nation!

DAY 10   Date:

I find that the harder I work,
the more luck I seem to have. —THOMAS JEFFERSON

I am grateful for:

In 90 days I will:

My #1 focus today is:

By the end of the day I will have accomplished these three measurable objectives that support my S.M.A.R.T. goal.

1.

2.

3.

Action plan for the day:

O

O

O

O

O

Thoughts/ideas/musings:

_____

_____

_____

_____

Recommended Resource: Asana: Teamwork without email. Asana puts conversations and tasks together, so you can get more done with less effort.

NIGHT 10

Two wonderful things that happened today:

1.

2.

Two struggles I encountered:

1.

2.

Possible solutions for these struggles:

1.

2.

Tomorrow will be a great day because:

_____

_____

_____

_____

_____

Final thought of the day:

_____

_____

_____

_____

_____

 Goodnight, Fire Nation!

GAUGING YOUR PACE

—10-DAY SPRINT RECAP—

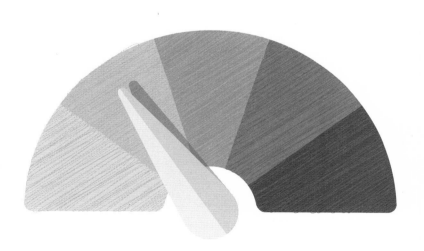

10-DAY SPRINT RECAP

My major accomplishment during this sprint:

_____

_____

_____

My two biggest struggles during this sprint:

1.

2.

Two possible solutions to these struggles:

1.

2.

_____

I want to put a ding in the universe. —STEVE JOBS

_____

Thoughts/ideas/musings:

_____

_____

_____

_____

_____

Fill in your current progress to your 100-day goal!   ⌐ BONUS ¬

  25%   50%   75%   100%   125%

CONGRATULATIONS!
YOU'VE COMPLETED 10% OF YOUR 100 DAYS!

ON YOUR MARK

— 10-DAY SPRINT —

SECOND 10-DAY SPRINT

The micro-goal I will accomplish during this sprint:

_____

_____

_____

Three specific actions I will take to accomplish this micro-goal:

1.

2.

3.

One habit I will implement over the next 10 days:

My action plan to implement this habit:

_____

_____

_____

DAY 11   Date:

Only put off until tomorrow what you are willing to die having left undone. —PABLO PICASSO

I am grateful for:

In 89 days I will:

My #1 focus today is:

By the end of the day I will have accomplished these three measurable objectives that support my S.M.A.R.T. goal.

1.

2.

3.

Action plan for the day:

○

○

○

○

○

Thoughts/ideas/musings:

_____

_____

_____

_____

Recommended Resource: Dropbox: Dropbox is a free service that lets you bring your photos, docs, and videos anywhere and share them easily. Never email yourself a file again!

NIGHT 11

Two wonderful things that happened today:

1.

2.

Two struggles I encountered:

1.

2.

Possible solutions for these struggles:

1.

2.

Tomorrow will be a great day because:

_____

_____

_____

_____

_____

Final thought of the day:

_____

_____

_____

_____

 Goodnight, Fire Nation!

DAY 12   Date:

Success is liking yourself, liking what you do, and liking how you do it. —MAYA ANGELOU

I am grateful for:

In 88 days I will:

My #1 focus today is:

By the end of the day I will have accomplished these three measurable objectives that support my S.M.A.R.T. goal.

1.

2.

3.

Action plan for the day:

O

O

O

O

O

Thoughts/ideas/musings:

_____

_____

_____

_____

Recommended Resource: MarcandAngel.com: Marc and Angel share practical tips and ideas on life, hacks, productivity, aspirations, health, work, tech and general self-improvement.

NIGHT 12

Two wonderful things that happened today:

1.

2.

Two struggles I encountered:

1.

2.

Possible solutions for these struggles:

1.

2.

Tomorrow will be a great day because:

_____

_____

_____

_____

_____

Final thought of the day:

_____

_____

_____

_____

_____

 Goodnight, Fire Nation!

DAY 13   Date:

Failure is often that early morning hour of darkness which precedes the dawning of the day of success. —LEIGH MITCHELL HODGES

I am grateful for:

In 87 days I will:

My #1 focus today is:

By the end of the day I will have accomplished these three measurable objectives that support my S.M.A.R.T. goal.

1.

2.

3.

Action plan for the day:

O

O

O

O

O

Thoughts/ideas/musings:

_____

_____

_____

_____

Recommended Resource: TaskRabbit: Get just about anything done by friendly, trustworthy people. Vetted TaskRabbits can help with errands, cleaning, delivery and so much more.

NIGHT 13

Two wonderful things that happened today:

1.

2.

Two struggles I encountered:

1.

2.

Possible solutions for these struggles:

1.

2.

Tomorrow will be a great day because:

_____

_____

_____

_____

_____

Final thought of the day:

_____

_____

_____

_____

 Goodnight, Fire Nation!

DAY 14   Date:

We become what we think about most of the time, and that's the strangest secret. —EARL NIGHTINGALE

I am grateful for:

In 86 days I will:

My #1 focus today is:

By the end of the day I will have accomplished these three measurable objectives that support my S.M.A.R.T. goal.

1.

2.

3.

Action plan for the day:

O

O

O

O

O

Thoughts/ideas/musings:

_____

_____

_____

_____

Recommended Resource: Coach.me: Coach.me employs coaching, community, and data to help you be your best. Stay motivated with guidance and encouragement.

NIGHT 14

Two wonderful things that happened today:

1.

2.

Two struggles I encountered:

1.

2.

Possible solutions for these struggles:

1.

2.

Tomorrow will be a great day because:

_____

_____

_____

_____

_____

Final thought of the day:

_____

_____

_____

_____

_____

 Goodnight, Fire Nation!

DAY 15   Date:

The only place where success comes before work is in the dictionary. —VIDAL SASSOON

I am grateful for:

In 85 days I will:

My #1 focus today is:

By the end of the day I will have accomplished these three measurable objectives that support my S.M.A.R.T. goal.

1.

2.

3.

Action plan for the day:

O

O

O

O

O

Thoughts/ideas/musings:

_____

_____

_____

_____

Recommended Resource: Trello: Infinitely flexible. Incredibly easy to use. Great mobile apps. It's free. Trello keeps track of everything, from the big picture to the minute details.

NIGHT 15

Two wonderful things that happened today:

1.

2.

Two struggles I encountered:

1.

2.

Possible solutions for these struggles:

1.

2.

Tomorrow will be a great day because:

_____
_____
_____
_____
_____

Final thought of the day:

_____
_____
_____
_____
_____

 Goodnight, Fire Nation!

DAY 16   Date:

Success is walking from failure to failure with no loss of enthusiasm. —WINSTON CHURCHILL

I am grateful for:

In 84 days I will:

My #1 focus today is:

By the end of the day I will have accomplished these three measurable objectives that support my S.M.A.R.T. goal.

1.

2.

3.

Action plan for the day:

O

O

O

O

O

Thoughts/ideas/musings:

_____

_____

_____

_____

Recommended Resource: ChrisBrogan.com: Chris Brogan is an American author, journalist, marketing consultant, and speaker about social media marketing.

NIGHT 16

Two wonderful things that happened today:

1.

2.

Two struggles I encountered:

1.

2.

Possible solutions for these struggles:

1.

2.

Tomorrow will be a great day because:

_____

_____

_____

_____

_____

Final thought of the day:

_____

_____

_____

_____

_____

 Goodnight, Fire Nation!

DAY 17   Date:

The successful warrior is the average man, with laser-like focus. —BRUCE LEE

I am grateful for:

In 83 days I will:

My #1 focus today is:

By the end of the day I will have accomplished these three measurable objectives that support my S.M.A.R.T. goal.

1.

2.

3.

Action plan for the day:

O

O

O

O

O

Thoughts/ideas/musings:

_____

_____

_____

_____

Recommended Resource: Rapportive: Rapportive shows you everything about your contacts right inside your inbox. They combine what you know, what your organization knows, and what the web contains.

NIGHT 17

Two wonderful things that happened today:

1.

2.

Two struggles I encountered:

1.

2.

Possible solutions for these struggles:

1.

2.

Tomorrow will be a great day because:

_____

_____

_____

_____

_____

Final thought of the day:

_____

_____

_____

_____

 Goodnight, Fire Nation!

DAY 18   Date:

Whenever you find yourself on the side of the majority, it is time to pause and reflect. —MARK TWAIN

I am grateful for:

In 82 days I will:

My #1 focus today is:

By the end of the day I will have accomplished these three measurable objectives that support my S.M.A.R.T. goal.

1.

2.

3.

Action plan for the day:

O

O

O

O

O

Thoughts/ideas/musings:

_____

_____

_____

_____

Recommended Resource: Vocaroo: Vocaroo is a quick and easy way to share voice messages over the internet.

NIGHT 18

Two wonderful things that happened today:

1.

2.

Two struggles I encountered:

1.

2.

Possible solutions for these struggles:

1.

2.

Tomorrow will be a great day because:

_____

_____

_____

_____

_____

Final thought of the day:

_____

_____

_____

_____

 Goodnight, Fire Nation!

DAY 19   Date:

Develop success from failures. Discouragement and failure are two of the surest stepping stones to success. —DALE CARNEGIE

I am grateful for:

In 81 days I will:

My #1 focus today is:

By the end of the day I will have accomplished these three measurable objectives that support my S.M.A.R.T. goal.

1.

2.

3.

Action plan for the day:

O

O

O

O

O

Thoughts/ideas/musings:

_____

_____

_____

_____

Recommended Resource: RescueTime: Helps you understand your daily habits so you can focus and be more productive.

NIGHT 19

Two wonderful things that happened today:

1.

2.

Two struggles I encountered:

1.

2.

Possible solutions for these struggles:

1.

2.

Tomorrow will be a great day because:

_____

_____

_____

_____

_____

Final thought of the day:

_____

_____

_____

_____

 Goodnight, Fire Nation!

DAY 20   Date:

Successful people do what unsuccessful people are not willing to do. Don't wish it were easier, wish you were better. —JIM ROHN

I am grateful for:

In 80 days I will:

My #1 focus today is:

By the end of the day I will have accomplished these three measurable objectives that support my S.M.A.R.T. goal.

1.

2.

3.

Action plan for the day:

O

O

O

O

O

Thoughts/ideas/musings:

_____

_____

_____

_____

Recommended Resource: AmyPorterfield.com: Amy Porterfield is a social media strategy consultant.

NIGHT 20

Two wonderful things that happened today:

1.

2.

Two struggles I encountered:

1.

2.

Possible solutions for these struggles:

1.

2.

Tomorrow will be a great day because:

_____

_____

_____

_____

_____

Final thought of the day:

_____

_____

_____

_____

_____

 Goodnight, Fire Nation!

GAUGING YOUR PACE
—10-DAY SPRINT RECAP—

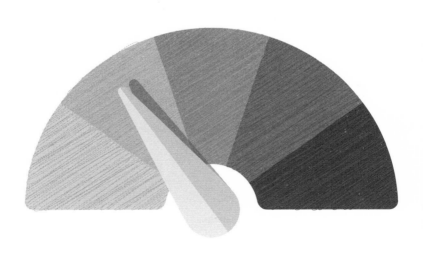

10-DAY SPRINT RECAP

My major accomplishment during this sprint:

_____

_____

_____

My two biggest struggles during this sprint:

1.

2.

Two possible solutions to these struggles:

1.

2.

_____

We become what we repeatedly do. —SEAN COVEY

_____

Thoughts/ideas/musings:

_____

_____

_____

_____

_____

Fill in your current progress to your 100-day goal!   ⌐ BONUS ¬

   25%   50%   75%   100%   125%

CONGRATULATIONS!
YOU'VE COMPLETED 20% OF YOUR 100 DAYS!

ON YOUR MARK

—10-DAY SPRINT—

START

THIRD 10-DAY SPRINT

The micro-goal I will accomplish during this sprint:

_____

_____

_____

Three specific actions I will take to accomplish this micro-goal:

1.

2.

3.

One habit I will implement over the next 10 days:

My action plan to implement this habit:

_____

_____

_____

DAY 21   Date:

You must expect great things of yourself before you can do them. —MICHAEL JORDAN

I am grateful for:

In 79 days I will:

My #1 focus today is:

By the end of the day I will have accomplished these three measurable objectives that support my S.M.A.R.T. goal.

1.

2.

3.

Action plan for the day:

O

O

O

O

O

Thoughts/ideas/musings:

_____

_____

_____

_____

Recommended Resource: Anti-Social: You know when you're trying to get work done, but end up wasting time on Facebook and Twitter? Anti-Social solves that problem.

NIGHT 21

Two wonderful things that happened today:

1.

2.

Two struggles I encountered:

1.

2.

Possible solutions for these struggles:

1.

2.

Tomorrow will be a great day because:

_____

_____

_____

_____

_____

Final thought of the day:

_____

_____

_____

_____

_____

 Goodnight, Fire Nation!

I don't want to get to the end of my life and find that I lived just the length of it. I want to have lived the width of it as well. —DIANE ACKERMAN

I am grateful for:

In 78 days I will:

My #1 focus today is:

By the end of the day I will have accomplished these three measurable objectives that support my S.M.A.R.T. goal.

1.

2.

3.

Action plan for the day:

O

O

O

O

O

Thoughts/ideas/musings:

_____

_____

_____

_____

Recommended Resource: TimeTrade: Online appointment scheduling by TimeTrade is used by businesses to create new sales prospects, accelerate the sales and service process, and make it easy.

NIGHT 22

Two wonderful things that happened today:

1.

2.

Two struggles I encountered:

1.

2.

Possible solutions for these struggles:

1.

2.

Tomorrow will be a great day because:

_____
_____
_____
_____
_____

Final thought of the day:

_____
_____
_____
_____
_____

 Goodnight, Fire Nation!

DAY 23   Date:

There is no chance, no destiny, no fate, that can hinder or control the firm resolve of a determined soul. —ELLA WHEELER WILCOX

I am grateful for:

In 77 days I will:

My #1 focus today is:

By the end of the day I will have accomplished these three measurable objectives that support my S.M.A.R.T. goal.

1.

2.

3.

Action plan for the day:

O

O

O

O

O

Thoughts/ideas/musings:

_____

_____

_____

_____

Recommended Resource: Wunderlist: The easiest way to organize your life and business, whether you're planning an overseas adventure or sharing a shopping list with a loved one.

NIGHT 23

Two wonderful things that happened today:

1.

2.

Two struggles I encountered:

1.

2.

Possible solutions for these struggles:

1.

2.

Tomorrow will be a great day because:

_____

_____

_____

_____

_____

Final thought of the day:

_____

_____

_____

_____

_____

 Goodnight, Fire Nation!

DAY 24 Date:

You've got to get up every morning with determination if you're going to go to bed with satisfaction. —GEORGE LORIMER

I am grateful for:

In 76 days I will:

My #1 focus today is:

By the end of the day I will have accomplished these three measurable objectives that support my S.M.A.R.T. goal.

1.

2.

3.

Action plan for the day:

○

○

○

○

○

Thoughts/ideas/musings:

_____

_____

_____

_____

Recommended Resource: The SmartPassiveIncome Blog: Learn how to build an online passive income business with Pat Flynn.

NIGHT 24

Two wonderful things that happened today:

1.

2.

Two struggles I encountered:

1.

2.

Possible solutions for these struggles:

1.

2.

Tomorrow will be a great day because:

_____

_____

_____

_____

_____

Final thought of the day:

_____

_____

_____

_____

_____

 Goodnight, Fire Nation!

DAY 25 Date:

Success is...knowing your purpose in life, growing to reach your maximum potential, and sowing seeds that benefit others. —JOHN C. MAXWELL

I am grateful for:

In 75 days I will:

My #1 focus today is:

By the end of the day I will have accomplished these three measurable objectives that support my S.M.A.R.T. goal.

1.

2.

3.

Action plan for the day:

O

O

O

O

O

Thoughts/ideas/musings:

_____

_____

_____

_____

Recommended Resource: LeadPages: The world's easiest landing page generator. It's the easiest way to build conversion optimized and mobile responsive landing pages.

NIGHT 25

Two wonderful things that happened today:

1.

2.

Two struggles I encountered:

1.

2.

Possible solutions for these struggles:

1.

2.

Tomorrow will be a great day because:

_____

_____

_____

_____

_____

Final thought of the day:

_____

_____

_____

_____

_____

 Goodnight, Fire Nation!

PAUSE FOR PERSPECTIVE

— QUARTERLY REVIEW —

FIRST QUARTERLY REVIEW

Big accomplishments in the last 25 days:

1.

2.

3.

Areas I need to improve in the next 25 days:

1.

2.

3.

I am proud that:

I am excited about:

I am surprised by:

Thoughts/ideas/musings:

_____

_____

_____

_____

_____

CONGRATULATIONS!
YOU'VE COMPLETED 25% OF YOUR 100 DAYS!

DAY 26 Date:

Be miserable. Or motivate yourself.
Whatever has to be done, it's always your choice. —WAYNE DYER

I am grateful for:

In 74 days I will:

My #1 focus today is:

By the end of the day I will have accomplished these three measurable objectives that support my S.M.A.R.T. goal.

1.

2.

3.

Action plan for the day:

O

O

O

O

O

Thoughts/ideas/musings:

_____

_____

_____

_____

Recommended Resource: ScreenFlow: With ScreenFlow you can record the contents of your entire monitor while also capturing your video camera, iOS device, microphone and your computer audio.

NIGHT 26

Two wonderful things that happened today:

1.

2.

Two struggles I encountered:

1.

2.

Possible solutions for these struggles:

1.

2.

Tomorrow will be a great day because:

_____

_____

_____

_____

_____

Final thought of the day:

_____

_____

_____

_____

 Goodnight, Fire Nation!

DAY 27 Date:

To accomplish great things, we must not only act, but also dream; not only plan, but also believe. —ANATOLE FRANCE

I am grateful for:

In 73 days I will:

My #1 focus today is:

By the end of the day I will have accomplished these three measurable objectives that support my S.M.A.R.T. goal.

1.

2.

3.

Action plan for the day:

○

○

○

○

○

Thoughts/ideas/musings:

_____

_____

_____

_____

Recommended Resource: Visual Website Optimizer: The world's easiest A/B testing tool.

93

NIGHT 27

Two wonderful things that happened today:

1.

2.

Two struggles I encountered:

1.

2.

Possible solutions for these struggles:

1.

2.

Tomorrow will be a great day because:

_____

_____

_____

_____

_____

Final thought of the day:

_____

_____

_____

_____

_____

 Goodnight, Fire Nation!

DAY 28 Date:

I attribute my success to this:
I never gave or took any excuse. —FLORENCE NIGHTINGALE

I am grateful for:

In 72 days I will:

My #1 focus today is:

By the end of the day I will have accomplished these three measurable objectives that support my S.M.A.R.T. goal.

1.

2.

3.

Action plan for the day:

O

O

O

O

O

Thoughts/ideas/musings:

_____

_____

_____

_____

Recommended Resource: HowToFascinate.com: Sally Hogshead is a world-class branding expert and best-selling author.

NIGHT 28

Two wonderful things that happened today:

1.

2.

Two struggles I encountered:

1.

2.

Possible solutions for these struggles:

1.

2.

Tomorrow will be a great day because:

_____

_____

_____

_____

_____

Final thought of the day:

_____

_____

_____

_____

_____

 Goodnight, Fire Nation!

DAY 29   Date:

The most difficult thing is the decision to act, the rest is merely tenacity. —AMELIA EARHART

I am grateful for:

In 71 days I will:

My #1 focus today is:

By the end of the day I will have accomplished these three measurable objectives that support my S.M.A.R.T. goal.

1.

2.

3.

Action plan for the day:

O

O

O

O

O

Thoughts/ideas/musings:

_____

_____

_____

_____

Recommended Resource: MindMeister: Create, share and collaboratively work on mind maps with MindMeister, the leading online mind mapping software. Includes apps for iPhone, iPad and Android.

NIGHT 29

Two wonderful things that happened today:

1.

2.

Two struggles I encountered:

1.

2.

Possible solutions for these struggles:

1.

2.

Tomorrow will be a great day because:

_____
_____
_____
_____
_____

Final thought of the day:

_____
_____
_____
_____
_____

 Goodnight, Fire Nation!

DAY 30 Date:

The mind is everything.
What you think you become. —BUDDHA

I am grateful for:

In 70 days I will:

My #1 focus today is:

By the end of the day I will have accomplished these three measurable objectives that support my S.M.A.R.T. goal.

1.

2.

3.

Action plan for the day:

O

O

O

O

O

Thoughts/ideas/musings:

_____

_____

_____

_____

Recommended Resource: TextExpander: Type more with less effort. TextExpander saves you time and keystrokes, expanding custom keyboard shortcuts into frequently used text and pictures.

NIGHT 30

Two wonderful things that happened today:

1.

2.

Two struggles I encountered:

1.

2.

Possible solutions for these struggles:

1.

2.

Tomorrow will be a great day because:

_____

_____

_____

_____

_____

Final thought of the day:

_____

_____

_____

_____

_____

 Goodnight, Fire Nation!

GAUGING YOUR PACE

—10-DAY SPRINT RECAP—

10-DAY SPRINT RECAP

My major accomplishment during this sprint:

_____

_____

_____

My two biggest struggles during this sprint:

1.

2.

Two possible solutions to these struggles:

1.

2.

_____

A leader is one who knows the way, goes the way, and shows the way. —JOHN C. MAXWELL

_____

Thoughts/ideas/musings:

_____

_____

_____

_____

_____

Fill in your current progress to your 100-day goal!   ⌐ BONUS ¬

25%   50%   75%   100%   125%

CONGRATULATIONS!
YOU'VE COMPLETED 30% OF YOUR 100 DAYS!

ON YOUR MARK

---- 10-DAY SPRINT ----

FOURTH 10-DAY SPRINT

The micro-goal I will accomplish during this sprint:

_____

_____

_____

Three specific actions I will take to accomplish this micro-goal:

1.

2.

3.

One habit I will implement over the next 10 days:

My action plan to implement this habit:

_____

_____

_____

DAY 31   Date:

The best time to plant a tree was twenty years ago.
The second best time is now. —CHINESE PROVERB

I am grateful for:

In 69 days I will:

My #1 focus today is:

By the end of the day I will have accomplished these three measurable objectives that support my S.M.A.R.T. goal.

1.

2.

3.

Action plan for the day:

○

○

○

○

○

Thoughts/ideas/musings:

_____

_____

_____

_____

Recommended Resource: Optimizely: Improve conversions through A/B testing, split testing and multivariate testing.

NIGHT 31

Two wonderful things that happened today:

1.

2.

Two struggles I encountered:

1.

2.

Possible solutions for these struggles:

1.

2.

Tomorrow will be a great day because:

_____

_____

_____

_____

_____

Final thought of the day:

_____

_____

_____

_____

_____

 Goodnight, Fire Nation!

DAY 32   Date:

Eighty percent of success is showing up. —WOODY ALLEN

I am grateful for:

In 68 days I will:

My #1 focus today is:

By the end of the day I will have accomplished these three measurable objectives that support my S.M.A.R.T. goal.

1.

2.

3.

Action plan for the day:

O

O

O

O

O

Thoughts/ideas/musings:

_____

_____

_____

_____

Recommended Resource: ViewFromTheTop.com: Aaron Walker is a business and life coach helping others discover what is vital to their business and their life.

NIGHT 32

Two wonderful things that happened today:

1.

2.

Two struggles I encountered:

1.

2.

Possible solutions for these struggles:

1.

2.

Tomorrow will be a great day because:

_____

_____

_____

_____

_____

Final thought of the day:

_____

_____

_____

_____

 Goodnight, Fire Nation!

DAY 33 Date:

I am not a product of my circumstances.
I am a product of my decisions. —STEPHEN COVEY

I am grateful for:

In 67 days I will:

My #1 focus today is:

By the end of the day I will have accomplished these three measurable objectives that support my S.M.A.R.T. goal.

1.

2.

3.

Action plan for the day:

O

O

O

O

O

Thoughts/ideas/musings:

_____

_____

_____

_____

Recommended Resource: PicMonkey: Edit photos, create collages, add text and more. Get PicMonkey Royale for ads-free editing plus access to primo effects.

NIGHT 33

Two wonderful things that happened today:

1.

2.

Two struggles I encountered:

1.

2.

Possible solutions for these struggles:

1.

2.

Tomorrow will be a great day because:

_____

_____

_____

_____

_____

Final thought of the day:

_____

_____

_____

_____

_____

 Goodnight, Fire Nation!

DAY 34 Date:

I've learned that people will forget what you said, people will forget what you did, but people will never forget how you made them feel. —MAYA ANGELOU

I am grateful for:

In 66 days I will:

My #1 focus today is:

By the end of the day I will have accomplished these three measurable objectives that support my S.M.A.R.T. goal.

1.

2.

3.

Action plan for the day:

O

O

O

O

O

Thoughts/ideas/musings:

_____

_____

_____

_____

Recommended Resource: Unroll.Me: Toss the junk with one click. After you sign up, see a list of all your subscription emails. Unsubscribe instantly from whatever you don't want.

NIGHT 34

Two wonderful things that happened today:

1.

2.

Two struggles I encountered:

1.

2.

Possible solutions for these struggles:

1.

2.

Tomorrow will be a great day because:

_____

_____

_____

_____

_____

Final thought of the day:

_____

_____

_____

_____

_____

 Goodnight, Fire Nation!

DAY 35 Date:

Either you run the day, or the day runs you. —JIM ROHN

I am grateful for:

In 65 days I will:

My #1 focus today is:

By the end of the day I will have accomplished these three measurable objectives that support my S.M.A.R.T. goal.

1.

2.

3.

Action plan for the day:

O

O

O

O

O

Thoughts/ideas/musings:

_____

_____

_____

_____

Recommended Resource: Virtual Staff Finder: A one-stop hub for hiring a virtual assistant.

NIGHT 35

Two wonderful things that happened today:

1.

2.

Two struggles I encountered:

1.

2.

Possible solutions for these struggles:

1.

2.

Tomorrow will be a great day because:

_____

_____

_____

_____

_____

Final thought of the day:

_____

_____

_____

_____

_____

 Goodnight, Fire Nation!

DAY 36 Date:

Whether you think you can, or you think you can't, you're right. —HENRY FORD

I am grateful for:

In 64 days I will:

My #1 focus today is:

By the end of the day I will have accomplished these three measurable objectives that support my S.M.A.R.T. goal.

1.

2.

3.

Action plan for the day:

O

O

O

O

O

Thoughts/ideas/musings:

_____
_____
_____
_____

Recommended Resource: HalElrod.com: Hal Elrod is a #1 best-selling author of *The Miracle Morning.*

NIGHT 36

Two wonderful things that happened today:

1.

2.

Two struggles I encountered:

1.

2.

Possible solutions for these struggles:

1.

2.

Tomorrow will be a great day because:

_____

_____

_____

_____

_____

Final thought of the day:

_____

_____

_____

_____

_____

 Goodnight, Fire Nation!

DAY 37 Date:

Whatever you can do, or dream you can, begin it. Boldness has genius, power and magic in it. —JOHANN WOLFGANG VON GOETHE

I am grateful for:

In 63 days I will:

My #1 focus today is:

By the end of the day I will have accomplished these three measurable objectives that support my S.M.A.R.T. goal.

1.

2.

3.

Action plan for the day:

O

O

O

O

O

Thoughts/ideas/musings:

_____
_____
_____
_____

Recommended Resource: Sleep Cycle: Using the accelerometer in your phone to monitor your movement during different sleep phases, Sleep Cycle tracks your sleep patterns and wakes you during your lightest sleep phase.

NIGHT 37

Two wonderful things that happened today:

1.

2.

Two struggles I encountered:

1.

2.

Possible solutions for these struggles:

1.

2.

Tomorrow will be a great day because:

_____

_____

_____

_____

_____

Final thought of the day:

_____

_____

_____

_____

_____

 Goodnight, Fire Nation!

DAY 38 Date:

There is only one way to avoid criticism: do nothing, say nothing, and be nothing. —ARISTOTLE

I am grateful for:

In 62 days I will:

My #1 focus today is:

By the end of the day I will have accomplished these three measurable objectives that support my S.M.A.R.T. goal.

1.

2.

3.

Action plan for the day:

○

○

○

○

○

Thoughts/ideas/musings:

_____

_____

_____

_____

Recommended Resource: KeePass: This free open source password manager helps you manage your passwords securely.

NIGHT 38

Two wonderful things that happened today:

1.

2.

Two struggles I encountered:

1.

2.

Possible solutions for these struggles:

1.

2.

Tomorrow will be a great day because:

_____

_____

_____

_____

_____

Final thought of the day:

_____

_____

_____

_____

 Goodnight, Fire Nation!

DAY 39   Date:

Go confidently in the direction of your dreams.
Live the life you have imagined. —HENRY DAVID THOREAU

I am grateful for:

In 61 days I will:

My #1 focus today is:

By the end of the day I will have accomplished these three measurable objectives that support my S.M.A.R.T. goal.

1.

2.

3.

Action plan for the day:

O

O

O

O

O

Thoughts/ideas/musings:

_____

_____

_____

_____

Recommended Resource: Zapier: Unlock the hidden power of your apps. Zapier connects the web apps you use to easily move your data and automate tedious tasks.

NIGHT 39

Two wonderful things that happened today:

1.

2.

Two struggles I encountered:

1.

2.

Possible solutions for these struggles:

1.

2.

Tomorrow will be a great day because:

_____

_____

_____

_____

_____

Final thought of the day:

_____

_____

_____

_____

 Goodnight, Fire Nation!

DAY 40 Date:

Start where you are. Use what you have.
Do what you can. —ARTHUR ASHE

I am grateful for:

In 60 days I will:

My #1 focus today is:

By the end of the day I will have accomplished these three measurable objectives that support my S.M.A.R.T. goal.

1.

2.

3.

Action plan for the day:

O

O

O

O

O

Thoughts/ideas/musings:

_____

_____

_____

_____

Recommended Resource: BoostBlogTraffic: Jon Morrow shares how to get more readers, become an authority in your niche, and get the attention you deserve.

NIGHT 40

Two wonderful things that happened today:

1.

2.

Two struggles I encountered:

1.

2.

Possible solutions for these struggles:

1.

2.

Tomorrow will be a great day because:

_____

_____

_____

_____

_____

Final thought of the day:

_____

_____

_____

_____

_____

 Goodnight, Fire Nation!

GAUGING YOUR PACE

—10-DAY SPRINT RECAP—

10-DAY SPRINT RECAP

My major accomplishment during this sprint:

_____

_____

_____

My two biggest struggles during this sprint:

1.

2.

Two possible solutions to these struggles:

1.

2.

_____

Successful people are simply those with successful habits. —BRIAN TRACY

_____

Thoughts/ideas/musings:

_____

_____

_____

_____

_____

Fill in your current progress to your 100-day goal!   ⌐ BONUS ⌐

25%	50%	75%	100%	125%

CONGRATULATIONS!
YOU'VE COMPLETED 40% OF YOUR 100 DAYS!

ON YOUR MARK

──── 10-DAY SPRINT ────

FIFTH 10-DAY SPRINT

The micro-goal I will accomplish during this sprint:

_____

_____

_____

Three specific actions I will take to accomplish this micro-goal:

1.

2.

3.

One habit I will implement over the next 10 days:

My action plan to implement this habit:

_____

_____

_____

DAY 41   Date:

How wonderful it is that nobody need wait a single moment before starting to improve the world. —ANNE FRANK

I am grateful for:

In 59 days I will:

My #1 focus today is:

By the end of the day I will have accomplished these three measurable objectives that support my S.M.A.R.T. goal.

1.

2.

3.

Action plan for the day:

O

O

O

O

O

Thoughts/ideas/musings:

_____
_____
_____
_____

Recommended Resource: Skitch: Get your point across with fewer words using annotation, shapes and sketches, so that your ideas become reality faster.

NIGHT 41

Two wonderful things that happened today:

1.

2.

Two struggles I encountered:

1.

2.

Possible solutions for these struggles:

1.

2.

Tomorrow will be a great day because:

_____
_____
_____
_____
_____

Final thought of the day:

_____
_____
_____
_____
_____

 Goodnight, Fire Nation!

DAY 42 Date:

There are no traffic jams along the extra mile. —ROGER STAUBACH

I am grateful for:

In 58 days I will:

My #1 focus today is:

By the end of the day I will have accomplished these three measurable objectives that support my S.M.A.R.T. goal.

1.

2.

3.

Action plan for the day:

O

O

O

O

O

Thoughts/ideas/musings:

_____

_____

_____

_____

Recommended Resource: ScheduleOnce: A sophisticated online scheduling platform that works in tandem with Google Calendar and supports your business in a wide range of scheduling scenarios.

NIGHT 42

Two wonderful things that happened today:

1.

2.

Two struggles I encountered:

1.

2.

Possible solutions for these struggles:

1.

2.

Tomorrow will be a great day because:

_____
_____
_____
_____
_____

Final thought of the day:

_____
_____
_____
_____
_____

 Goodnight, Fire Nation!

DAY 43 Date:

Build your own dreams, or someone else will hire you to build theirs. —FARRAH GRAY

I am grateful for:

In 57 days I will:

My #1 focus today is:

By the end of the day I will have accomplished these three measurable objectives that support my S.M.A.R.T. goal.

1.

2.

3.

Action plan for the day:

O

O

O

O

O

Thoughts/ideas/musings:

_____

_____

_____

_____

Recommended Resource: Contactually: This web-based CRM tool will help maximize your network ROI.

NIGHT 43

Two wonderful things that happened today:

1.

2.

Two struggles I encountered:

1.

2.

Possible solutions for these struggles:

1.

2.

Tomorrow will be a great day because:

_____

_____

_____

_____

_____

Final thought of the day:

_____

_____

_____

_____

 Goodnight, Fire Nation!

DAY 44 Date:

Do what you can, with what you have, where you are. —TEDDY ROOSEVELT

I am grateful for:

In 56 days I will:

My #1 focus today is:

By the end of the day I will have accomplished these three measurable objectives that support my S.M.A.R.T. goal.

1.

2.

3.

Action plan for the day:

O

O

O

O

O

Thoughts/ideas/musings:

_____

_____

_____

_____

Recommended Resource: Ziglar.com: Ziglar strives to be the difference-maker in people's personal, family and professional success.

NIGHT 44

Two wonderful things that happened today:

1.

2.

Two struggles I encountered:

1.

2.

Possible solutions for these struggles:

1.

2.

Tomorrow will be a great day because:

_____

_____

_____

_____

_____

Final thought of the day:

_____

_____

_____

_____

_____

 Goodnight, Fire Nation!

DAY 45 Date:

You must find the place inside yourself where nothing is impossible. —DEEPAK CHOPRA

I am grateful for:

In 55 days I will:

My #1 focus today is:

By the end of the day I will have accomplished these three measurable objectives that support my S.M.A.R.T. goal.

1.

2.

3.

Action plan for the day:

O

O

O

O

O

Thoughts/ideas/musings:

_____

_____

_____

_____

Recommended Resource: IFTTT: Put the internet to work for you.

NIGHT 45

Two wonderful things that happened today:

1.

2.

Two struggles I encountered:

1.

2.

Possible solutions for these struggles:

1.

2.

Tomorrow will be a great day because:

_____

_____

_____

_____

_____

Final thought of the day:

_____

_____

_____

_____

_____

 Goodnight, Fire Nation!

DAY 46   Date:

You may be disappointed if you fail, but you are doomed if you don't try. —BEVERLY SILLS

I am grateful for:

In 54 days I will:

My #1 focus today is:

By the end of the day I will have accomplished these three measurable objectives that support my S.M.A.R.T. goal.

1.

2.

3.

Action plan for the day:

O

O

O

O

O

Thoughts/ideas/musings:

_____

_____

_____

_____

Recommended Resource: Post Planner: Free up 2 hours daily with Post Planner's powerhouse Post Scheduler for Facebook. Never run out of Like-worthy posts.

NIGHT 46

Two wonderful things that happened today:

1.

2.

Two struggles I encountered:

1.

2.

Possible solutions for these struggles:

1.

2.

Tomorrow will be a great day because:

_____
_____
_____
_____
_____

Final thought of the day:

_____
_____
_____
_____

 Goodnight, Fire Nation!

DAY 47 Date:

It's not the years in your life that count.
It's the life in your years. —ABRAHAM LINCOLN

I am grateful for:

In 53 days I will:

My #1 focus today is:

By the end of the day I will have accomplished these three measurable objectives that support my S.M.A.R.T. goal.

1.

2.

3.

Action plan for the day:

O

O

O

O

O

Thoughts/ideas/musings:

_____

_____

_____

_____

Recommended Resource: Clarity.fm: Get on-demand business advice from experts, and make faster and better decisions to grow your business.

NIGHT 47

Two wonderful things that happened today:

1.

2.

Two struggles I encountered:

1.

2.

Possible solutions for these struggles:

1.

2.

Tomorrow will be a great day because:

_____

_____

_____

_____

_____

Final thought of the day:

_____

_____

_____

_____

_____

 Goodnight, Fire Nation!

DAY 48   Date:

The past is history. The future is a mystery.
The present is a gift. —LISA UNGER

I am grateful for:

In 52 days I will:

My #1 focus today is:

By the end of the day I will have accomplished these three measurable objectives that support my S.M.A.R.T. goal.

1.

2.

3.

Action plan for the day:

○

○

○

○

○

Thoughts/ideas/musings:

_____

_____

_____

_____

Recommended Resource: JonathanFields.com: Jonathan is on a quest to create and curate ideas, stories and tools that'll help you come alive.

NIGHT 48

Two wonderful things that happened today:

1.

2.

Two struggles I encountered:

1.

2.

Possible solutions for these struggles:

1.

2.

Tomorrow will be a great day because:

_____

_____

_____

_____

_____

Final thought of the day:

_____

_____

_____

_____

_____

 Goodnight, Fire Nation!

DAY 49   Date:

If you are not embarrassed by the first version of your product, you've launched too late. —REID HOFFMAN

I am grateful for:

In 51 days I will:

My #1 focus today is:

By the end of the day I will have accomplished these three measurable objectives that support my S.M.A.R.T. goal.

1.

2.

3.

Action plan for the day:

○

○

○

○

○

Thoughts/ideas/musings:

_____

_____

_____

_____

Recommended Resource: Feedly: All your favorite websites in one place. Instead of having to hunt down news, Feedly aggregates and delivers the content of your favorite sites.

NIGHT 49

Two wonderful things that happened today:

1.

2.

Two struggles I encountered:

1.

2.

Possible solutions for these struggles:

1.

2.

Tomorrow will be a great day because:

_____

_____

_____

_____

_____

Final thought of the day:

_____

_____

_____

_____

_____

 Goodnight, Fire Nation!

DAY 50 Date:

What the mind can conceive and believe, the mind can achieve. —NAPOLEON HILL

I am grateful for:

In 50 days I will:

My #1 focus today is:

By the end of the day I will have accomplished these three measurable objectives that support my S.M.A.R.T. goal.

1.

2.

3.

Action plan for the day:

O

O

O

O

O

Thoughts/ideas/musings:

_____

_____

_____

_____

Recommended Resource: SelfControl: A free and open-source application for Mac OS X (10.5 or above) that lets you block your own access to distracting websites, your mail servers, etc.

NIGHT 50

Two wonderful things that happened today:

1.

2.

Two struggles I encountered:

1.

2.

Possible solutions for these struggles:

1.

2.

Tomorrow will be a great day because:

_____

_____

_____

_____

_____

Final thought of the day:

_____

_____

_____

_____

_____

 Goodnight, Fire Nation!

GAUGING YOUR PACE
—10-DAY SPRINT RECAP—

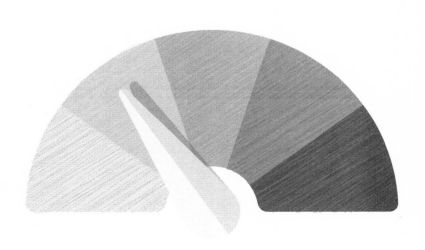

10-DAY SPRINT RECAP

My major accomplishment during this sprint:

_____

_____

_____

My two biggest struggles during this sprint:

1.

2.

Two possible solutions to these struggles:

1.

2.

_____

The chains of habit are generally too weak to be felt until they are too strong to be broken. —SAMUEL JOHNSON

_____

Thoughts/ideas/musings:

_____

_____

_____

_____

_____

Fill in your current progress to your 100-day goal!   ⌐ BONUS ¬

25%   50%   75%   100%   125%

CONGRATULATIONS!
YOU'VE COMPLETED 50% OF YOUR 100 DAYS!

PAUSE FOR PERSPECTIVE

— QUARTERLY REVIEW —

SECOND QUARTERLY REVIEW

Big accomplishments in the last 25 days:

1.

2.

3.

Areas I need to improve in the next 25 days:

1.

2.

3.

I am proud that:

I am excited about:

I am surprised by:

Thoughts/ideas/musings:

_____
_____
_____
_____
_____

CONGRATULATIONS!
YOU'VE COMPLETED 50% OF YOUR 100 DAYS!

ON YOUR MARK

—— 10-DAY SPRINT ——

SIXTH 10-DAY SPRINT

The micro-goal I will accomplish during this sprint:

_____

_____

_____

Three specific actions I will take to accomplish this micro-goal:

1.

2.

3.

One habit I will implement over the next 10 days:

My action plan to implement this habit:

_____

_____

_____

It's time to IGNITE!

DAY 51 Date:

Never mistake activity for achievement. —COACH JOHN WOODEN

I am grateful for:

In 49 days I will:

My #1 focus today is:

By the end of the day I will have accomplished these three measurable objectives that support my S.M.A.R.T. goal.

1.

2.

3.

Action plan for the day:

O

O

O

O

O

Thoughts/ideas/musings:

_____

_____

_____

_____

Recommended Resource: Pocket: Save for later. Put articles, videos or pretty much anything into Pocket. Save directly from your browser or from apps like Twitter, Flipboard, Pulse and Zite.

NIGHT 51

Two wonderful things that happened today:

1.

2.

Two struggles I encountered:

1.

2.

Possible solutions for these struggles:

1.

2.

Tomorrow will be a great day because:

_____

_____

_____

_____

_____

Final thought of the day:

_____

_____

_____

_____

_____

 Goodnight, Fire Nation!

DAY 52   Date:

The most powerful force on earth is the human soul on fire. —FERDINAND FOCH

I am grateful for:

In 48 days I will:

My #1 focus today is:

By the end of the day I will have accomplished these three measurable objectives that support my S.M.A.R.T. goal.

1.

2.

3.

Action plan for the day:

O

O

O

O

O

Thoughts/ideas/musings:

_____

_____

_____

_____

Recommended Resource: LewisHowes.com: Lewis will show you how to do what you love full time.

NIGHT 52

Two wonderful things that happened today:

1.

2.

Two struggles I encountered:

1.

2.

Possible solutions for these struggles:

1.

2.

Tomorrow will be a great day because:

_____
_____
_____
_____
_____

Final thought of the day:

_____
_____
_____
_____
_____

 Goodnight, Fire Nation!

DAY 53 Date:

We first make our habits, then our habits make us. —JOHN DRYDEN

I am grateful for:

In 47 days I will:

My #1 focus today is:

By the end of the day I will have accomplished these three measurable objectives that support my S.M.A.R.T. goal.

1.

2.

3.

Action plan for the day:

O

O

O

O

O

Thoughts/ideas/musings:

_____

_____

_____

_____

Recommended Resource: Mint: Does all the work of organizing and categorizing your spending for you. See where every dime goes.

NIGHT 53

Two wonderful things that happened today:

1.

2.

Two struggles I encountered:

1.

2.

Possible solutions for these struggles:

1.

2.

Tomorrow will be a great day because:

_____

_____

_____

_____

_____

Final thought of the day:

_____

_____

_____

_____

_____

 Goodnight, Fire Nation!

DAY 54 Date:

Even if you're on the right track,
you'll get run over if you just sit there. —WILL ROGERS

I am grateful for:

In 46 days I will:

My #1 focus today is:

By the end of the day I will have accomplished these three measurable objectives that support my S.M.A.R.T. goal.

1.

2.

3.

Action plan for the day:

O

O

O

O

O

Thoughts/ideas/musings:

_____

_____

_____

_____

Recommended Resource: TripIt: This travel organizing app keeps all of your travel plans in one spot. Create a master itinerary, and access your travel plans on any device.

NIGHT 54

Two wonderful things that happened today:

1.

2.

Two struggles I encountered:

1.

2.

Possible solutions for these struggles:

1.

2.

Tomorrow will be a great day because:

_____
_____
_____
_____
_____

Final thought of the day:

_____
_____
_____
_____
_____

 Goodnight, Fire Nation!

DAY 55   Date:

It is good to have an end to journey toward; but it is the journey that matters, in the end. —ERNEST HEMINGWAY

I am grateful for:

In 45 days I will:

My #1 focus today is:

By the end of the day I will have accomplished these three measurable objectives that support my S.M.A.R.T. goal.

1.

2.

3.

Action plan for the day:

O

O

O

O

O

Thoughts/ideas/musings:

_____

_____

_____

_____

Recommended Resource: AudioBooks: Download audiobooks online. Visit EOFireBook.com for a free audiobook today!

NIGHT 55

Two wonderful things that happened today:

1.

2.

Two struggles I encountered:

1.

2.

Possible solutions for these struggles:

1.

2.

Tomorrow will be a great day because:

_____
_____
_____
_____
_____

Final thought of the day:

_____
_____
_____
_____
_____

 Goodnight, Fire Nation!

DAY 56 Date:

Why you? Because there's no one better. Why now? Because tomorrow isn't soon enough. —DONNA BRAZILE

I am grateful for:

In 44 days I will:

My #1 focus today is:

By the end of the day I will have accomplished these three measurable objectives that support my S.M.A.R.T. goal.

1.

2.

3.

Action plan for the day:

O

O

O

O

O

Thoughts/ideas/musings:

_____

_____

_____

_____

Recommended Resource: SimpleGreenSmoothies.com: This website is full of green smoothie recipes so you can transform your body from the inside out.

NIGHT 56

Two wonderful things that happened today:

1.

2.

Two struggles I encountered:

1.

2.

Possible solutions for these struggles:

1.

2.

Tomorrow will be a great day because:

_____

_____

_____

_____

_____

Final thought of the day:

_____

_____

_____

_____

 Goodnight, Fire Nation!

DAY 57 Date:

Through perseverance many people win success out of what seemed destined to be certain failure. —BENJAMIN DISRAELI

I am grateful for:

In 43 days I will:

My #1 focus today is:

By the end of the day I will have accomplished these three measurable objectives that support my S.M.A.R.T. goal.

1.

2.

3.

Action plan for the day:

O

O

O

O

O

Thoughts/ideas/musings:

_____

_____

_____

_____

Recommended Resource: SaneBox: SaneBox intelligently analyzes your emails and filters your inbox of spam and unimportant messages.

NIGHT 57

Two wonderful things that happened today:

1.

2.

Two struggles I encountered:

1.

2.

Possible solutions for these struggles:

1.

2.

Tomorrow will be a great day because:

_____

_____

_____

_____

_____

Final thought of the day:

_____

_____

_____

_____

_____

 Goodnight, Fire Nation!

DAY 58 Date:

The way to get started is to
quit talking and begin doing. —WALT DISNEY

I am grateful for:

In 42 days I will:

My #1 focus today is:

By the end of the day I will have accomplished these three measurable
objectives that support my S.M.A.R.T. goal.

1.

2.

3.

Action plan for the day:

○

○

○

○

○

Thoughts/ideas/musings:

_____

_____

_____

_____

Recommended Resource: DocuSign: Securely sign and manage
documents online from any device with the most widely used
e-signature solution.

NIGHT 58

Two wonderful things that happened today:

1.

2.

Two struggles I encountered:

1.

2.

Possible solutions for these struggles:

1.

2.

Tomorrow will be a great day because:

_____

_____

_____

_____

_____

Final thought of the day:

_____

_____

_____

_____

_____

 Goodnight, Fire Nation!

DAY 59   Date:

You have within you, right now, everything you need to deal with whatever the world can throw at you. —BRIAN TRACY

I am grateful for:

In 41 days I will:

My #1 focus today is:

By the end of the day I will have accomplished these three measurable objectives that support my S.M.A.R.T. goal.

1.

2.

3.

Action plan for the day:

O

O

O

O

O

Thoughts/ideas/musings:

_____

_____

_____

_____

Recommended Resource: Upwork: Find freelancers and freelance jobs on Upwork, the world's largest online workplace, where savvy businesses and professional freelancers go to work.

NIGHT 59

Two wonderful things that happened today:

1.

2.

Two struggles I encountered:

1.

2.

Possible solutions for these struggles:

1.

2.

Tomorrow will be a great day because:

_____
_____
_____
_____
_____

Final thought of the day:

_____
_____
_____
_____
_____

 Goodnight, Fire Nation!

DAY 60 Date:

A happy person is not a person in a certain set of circumstances, but rather a person with a certain set of attitudes. —HUGH DOWNS

I am grateful for:

In 40 days I will:

My #1 focus today is:

By the end of the day I will have accomplished these three measurable objectives that support my S.M.A.R.T. goal.

1.

2.

3.

Action plan for the day:

○

○

○

○

○

Thoughts/ideas/musings:

_____

_____

_____

_____

Recommended Resource: LiveYourLegend.net: Scott Dinsmore shares how to change the world by doing work you love.

NIGHT 60

Two wonderful things that happened today:

1.

2.

Two struggles I encountered:

1.

2.

Possible solutions for these struggles:

1.

2.

Tomorrow will be a great day because:

_____

_____

_____

_____

_____

Final thought of the day:

_____

_____

_____

_____

 Goodnight, Fire Nation!

GAUGING YOUR PACE

—10-DAY SPRINT RECAP—

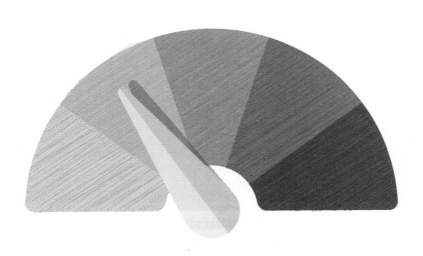

10-DAY SPRINT RECAP

My major accomplishment during this sprint:

_____

_____

_____

My two biggest struggles during this sprint:

1.

2.

Two possible solutions to these struggles:

1.

2.

We are what we repeatedly do.
Excellence, then, is not an act, but a habit. —ARISTOTLE

Thoughts/ideas/musings:

_____

_____

_____

_____

_____

Fill in your current progress to your 100-day goal! ⌐ BONUS ⌐

25%	50%	75%	100%	125%

CONGRATULATIONS!
YOU'VE COMPLETED 60% OF YOUR 100 DAYS!

ON YOUR MARK

— 10-DAY SPRINT —

SEVENTH 10-DAY SPRINT

The micro-goal I will accomplish during this sprint:

_____

_____

_____

Three specific actions I will take to accomplish this micro-goal:

1.

2.

3.

One habit I will implement over the next 10 days:

My action plan to implement this habit:

_____

_____

_____

DAY 61 Date:

Four things come not back: the spoken word, the sped arrow, the past life, and the neglected opportunity. —PROVERB

I am grateful for:

In 39 days I will:

My #1 focus today is:

By the end of the day I will have accomplished these three measurable objectives that support my S.M.A.R.T. goal.

1.

2.

3.

Action plan for the day:

○

○

○

○

○

Thoughts/ideas/musings:

_____

_____

_____

_____

Recommended Resource: Meetup.com: Helps groups of people with shared interests plan events and facilitates offline group meetings in various localities around the world.

NIGHT 61

Two wonderful things that happened today:

1.

2.

Two struggles I encountered:

1.

2.

Possible solutions for these struggles:

1.

2.

Tomorrow will be a great day because:

_____

_____

_____

_____

_____

Final thought of the day:

_____

_____

_____

_____

_____

 Goodnight, Fire Nation!

DAY 62   Date:

Most people don't recognize opportunity because it's dressed in overalls and looks like work. —THOMAS EDISON

I am grateful for:

In 38 days I will:

My #1 focus today is:

By the end of the day I will have accomplished these three measurable objectives that support my S.M.A.R.T. goal.

1.

2.

3.

Action plan for the day:

○

○

○

○

○

Thoughts/ideas/musings:

_____

_____

_____

_____

Recommended Resource: Headspace: A course of guided meditation, delivered via an app or online. Try Headspace's starter course, Take10, for free today.

NIGHT 62

Two wonderful things that happened today:

1.

2.

Two struggles I encountered:

1.

2.

Possible solutions for these struggles:

1.

2.

Tomorrow will be a great day because:

_____
_____
_____
_____
_____

Final thought of the day:

_____
_____
_____
_____
_____

 Goodnight, Fire Nation!

DAY 63   Date:

It's wonderful what we can do
if we're always doing. —GEORGE WASHINGTON

I am grateful for:

In 37 days I will:

My #1 focus today is:

By the end of the day I will have accomplished these three measurable objectives that support my S.M.A.R.T. goal.

1.

2.

3.

Action plan for the day:

○

○

○

○

○

Thoughts/ideas/musings:

_____

_____

_____

_____

Recommended Resource: OmmWriter: A simple text processor that's all about making writing pleasurable again.

NIGHT 63

Two wonderful things that happened today:

1.

2.

Two struggles I encountered:

1.

2.

Possible solutions for these struggles:

1.

2.

Tomorrow will be a great day because:

_____
_____
_____
_____
_____

Final thought of the day:

_____
_____
_____
_____
_____

 Goodnight, Fire Nation!

DAY 64 Date:

How does a project get to be a year behind schedule?
One day at a time. —FRED BROOKS

I am grateful for:

In 36 days I will:

My #1 focus today is:

By the end of the day I will have accomplished these three measurable objectives that support my S.M.A.R.T. goal.

1.

2.

3.

Action plan for the day:

○

○

○

○

○

Thoughts/ideas/musings:

_____

_____

_____

_____

Recommended Resource: Fizzle.co: Training from experts you trust and access to a virtual community of like-minded entrepreneurs.

NIGHT 64

Two wonderful things that happened today:

1.

2.

Two struggles I encountered:

1.

2.

Possible solutions for these struggles:

1.

2.

Tomorrow will be a great day because:

_____

_____

_____

_____

_____

Final thought of the day:

_____

_____

_____

_____

 Goodnight, Fire Nation!

DAY 65 Date:

Happiness is essentially a state of going somewhere, wholeheartedly, one-directionally, without regret or reservation. —WILLIAM H. SHELDON

I am grateful for:

In 35 days I will:

My #1 focus today is:

By the end of the day I will have accomplished these three measurable objectives that support my S.M.A.R.T. goal.

1.

2.

3.

Action plan for the day:

◯

◯

◯

◯

◯

Thoughts/ideas/musings:

_____

_____

_____

_____

Recommended Resource: Lucidchart: A visual collaboration tool that makes diagramming fast and easy.

NIGHT 65

Two wonderful things that happened today:

1.

2.

Two struggles I encountered:

1.

2.

Possible solutions for these struggles:

1.

2.

Tomorrow will be a great day because:

_____

_____

_____

_____

_____

Final thought of the day:

_____

_____

_____

_____

_____

 Goodnight, Fire Nation!

DAY 66 Date:

There is no such thing as a good idea unless it is developed and utilized. —KEKICH CREDO

I am grateful for:

In 34 days I will:

My #1 focus today is:

By the end of the day I will have accomplished these three measurable objectives that support my S.M.A.R.T. goal.

1.

2.

3.

Action plan for the day:

O

O

O

O

O

Thoughts/ideas/musings:

_____

_____

_____

_____

Recommended Resource: Meet Edgar: The only app that stops social media updates from going to waste.

NIGHT 66

Two wonderful things that happened today:

1.

2.

Two struggles I encountered:

1.

2.

Possible solutions for these struggles:

1.

2.

Tomorrow will be a great day because:

_____

_____

_____

_____

_____

Final thought of the day:

_____

_____

_____

_____

 Goodnight, Fire Nation!

DAY 67 Date:

Destiny is not a thing to be waited for, but a thing to be achieved. —WILLIAM JENNINGS BRYAN

I am grateful for:

In 33 days I will:

My #1 focus today is:

By the end of the day I will have accomplished these three measurable objectives that support my S.M.A.R.T. goal.

1.

2.

3.

Action plan for the day:

O

O

O

O

O

Thoughts/ideas/musings:

_____

_____

_____

_____

Recommended Resource: Fancy Hands: A team of assistants ready to work for you now. For a low monthly membership fee, you'll finally get the help you need.

NIGHT 67

Two wonderful things that happened today:

1.

2.

Two struggles I encountered:

1.

2.

Possible solutions for these struggles:

1.

2.

Tomorrow will be a great day because:

_____

_____

_____

_____

_____

Final thought of the day:

_____

_____

_____

_____

_____

 Goodnight, Fire Nation!

DAY 68   Date:

Keep away from people who try to belittle your ambitions. Small people always do that, but the really great make you feel that you, too, can become great. —MARK TWAIN

I am grateful for:

In 32 days I will:

My #1 focus today is:

By the end of the day I will have accomplished these three measurable objectives that support my S.M.A.R.T. goal.

1.

2.

3.

Action plan for the day:

O

O

O

O

O

Thoughts/ideas/musings:

_____

_____

_____

_____

Recommended Resource: SuperHumanEntrepreneur.com: Dr. Issac Jones guides the minds and spirits of entrepreneurs.

NIGHT 68

Two wonderful things that happened today:

1.

2.

Two struggles I encountered:

1.

2.

Possible solutions for these struggles:

1.

2.

Tomorrow will be a great day because:

_____

_____

_____

_____

_____

Final thought of the day:

_____

_____

_____

_____

_____

 Goodnight, Fire Nation!

DAY 69   Date:

The successful person has the habit of doing the things failures don't like to do. —THOMAS EDISON

I am grateful for:

In 31 days I will:

My #1 focus today is:

By the end of the day I will have accomplished these three measurable objectives that support my S.M.A.R.T. goal.

1.

2.

3.

Action plan for the day:

○

○

○

○

○

Thoughts/ideas/musings:

_____

_____

_____

_____

Recommended Resource: iDoneThis: An incredible management tool that provides unprecedented visibility into your productivity and areas for improvement.

NIGHT 69

Two wonderful things that happened today:

1.

2.

Two struggles I encountered:

1.

2.

Possible solutions for these struggles:

1.

2.

Tomorrow will be a great day because:

_____

_____

_____

_____

_____

Final thought of the day:

_____

_____

_____

_____

_____

 Goodnight, Fire Nation!

DAY 70   Date:

Things may come to those who wait, but only the things left by those who hustle. —ABRAHAM LINCOLN

I am grateful for:

In 30 days I will:

My #1 focus today is:

By the end of the day I will have accomplished these three measurable objectives that support my S.M.A.R.T. goal.

1.

2.

3.

Action plan for the day:

O

O

O

O

O

Thoughts/ideas/musings:

_____

_____

_____

_____

Recommended Resource: Zirtual: A virtual executive assistant service that matches busy people with dedicated personal assistants.

NIGHT 70

Two wonderful things that happened today:

1.

2.

Two struggles I encountered:

1.

2.

Possible solutions for these struggles:

1.

2.

Tomorrow will be a great day because:

_____
_____
_____
_____
_____

Final thought of the day:

_____
_____
_____
_____
_____

 Goodnight, Fire Nation!

GAUGING YOUR PACE

—10-DAY SPRINT RECAP—

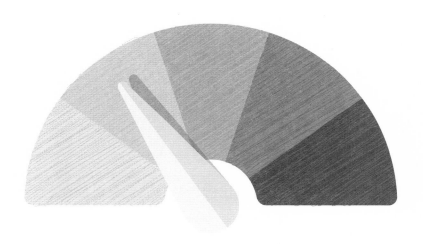

10-DAY SPRINT RECAP

My major accomplishment during this sprint:

_____

_____

_____

My two biggest struggles during this sprint:

1.

2.

Two possible solutions to these struggles:

1.

2.

_____

Ninety-nine percent of the failures come from people who have the habit of making excuses. —GEORGE WASHINGTON CARVER

_____

Thoughts/ideas/musings:

_____

_____

_____

_____

_____

Fill in your current progress to your 100-day goal!   ⌐ BONUS ¬

25%   50%   75%   100%   125%

CONGRATULATIONS!
YOU'VE COMPLETED 70% OF YOUR 100 DAYS!

ON YOUR MARK

—— 10-DAY SPRINT ——

EIGHTH 10-DAY SPRINT

The micro-goal I will accomplish during this sprint:

_____

_____

_____

Three specific actions I will take to accomplish this micro-goal:

1.

2.

3.

One habit I will implement over the next 10 days:

My action plan to implement this habit:

_____

_____

_____

It's time to IGNITE!

DAY 71   Date:

The most creative act you will ever undertake is the act of creating yourself. —DEEPAK CHOPRA

I am grateful for:

In 29 days I will:

My #1 focus today is:

By the end of the day I will have accomplished these three measurable objectives that support my S.M.A.R.T. goal.

1.

2.

3.

Action plan for the day:

O

O

O

O

O

Thoughts/ideas/musings:

_____

_____

_____

_____

Recommended Resource: Sprout Social: A social media management tool created to help businesses find new customers and grow their social media presence.

NIGHT 71

Two wonderful things that happened today:

1.

2.

Two struggles I encountered:

1.

2.

Possible solutions for these struggles:

1.

2.

Tomorrow will be a great day because:

_____

_____

_____

_____

_____

Final thought of the day:

_____

_____

_____

_____

_____

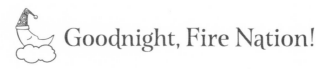 Goodnight, Fire Nation!

DAY 72   Date:

The height of your accomplishments is determined by the depth of your convictions. —WILLIAM F. SCOLAVINO

I am grateful for:

In 28 days I will:

My #1 focus today is:

By the end of the day I will have accomplished these three measurable objectives that support my S.M.A.R.T. goal.

1.

2.

3.

Action plan for the day:

○

○

○

○

○

Thoughts/ideas/musings:

_____

_____

_____

_____

Recommended Resource: TheShawnStevensonModel.com: Shawn's mission is to help you become the strongest, healthiest, happiest version of yourself.

NIGHT 72

Two wonderful things that happened today:

1.

2.

Two struggles I encountered:

1.

2.

Possible solutions for these struggles:

1.

2.

Tomorrow will be a great day because:

_____

_____

_____

_____

_____

Final thought of the day:

_____

_____

_____

_____

_____

 Goodnight, Fire Nation!

DAY 73   Date:

Discipline is the bridge between
goals and accomplishment. —JIM ROHN

I am grateful for:

In 27 days I will:

My #1 focus today is:

By the end of the day I will have accomplished these three measurable objectives that support my S.M.A.R.T. goal.

1.

2.

3.

Action plan for the day:

○

○

○

○

○

Thoughts/ideas/musings:

_____
_____
_____
_____

Recommended Resource: TeuxDeux: A bare-bones, but visually compelling and highly usable to-do app.

NIGHT 73

Two wonderful things that happened today:

1.

2.

Two struggles I encountered:

1.

2.

Possible solutions for these struggles:

1.

2.

Tomorrow will be a great day because:

_____
_____
_____
_____
_____

Final thought of the day:

_____
_____
_____
_____
_____

 Goodnight, Fire Nation!

DAY 74   Date:

Good habits are worth being fanatical about. —JOHN IRVING

I am grateful for:

In 26 days I will:

My #1 focus today is:

By the end of the day I will have accomplished these three measurable objectives that support my S.M.A.R.T. goal.

1.

2.

3.

Action plan for the day:

○

○

○

○

○

Thoughts/ideas/musings:

_____
_____
_____
_____

Recommended Resource: Boomerang: Adds scheduled sending and the easiest, most integrated email reminders to Gmail, helping you reach Inbox Zero.

NIGHT 74

Two wonderful things that happened today:

1.

2.

Two struggles I encountered:

1.

2.

Possible solutions for these struggles:

1.

2.

Tomorrow will be a great day because:

_____

_____

_____

_____

_____

Final thought of the day:

_____

_____

_____

_____

 Goodnight, Fire Nation!

DAY 75   Date:

The trouble with being punctual is that nobody's there to appreciate it. —FRANKLIN P. JONES

I am grateful for:

In 25 days I will:

My #1 focus today is:

By the end of the day I will have accomplished these three measurable objectives that support my S.M.A.R.T. goal.

1.

2.

3.

Action plan for the day:

O

O

O

O

O

Thoughts/ideas/musings:

_____

_____

_____

_____

Recommended Resource: Eventbrite: Brings people together through live experiences. Discover events that match your passions, or create your own with online ticketing tools.

NIGHT 75

Two wonderful things that happened today:

1.

2.

Two struggles I encountered:

1.

2.

Possible solutions for these struggles:

1.

2.

Tomorrow will be a great day because:

_____

_____

_____

_____

_____

Final thought of the day:

_____

_____

_____

_____

_____

 Goodnight, Fire Nation!

PAUSE FOR PERSPECTIVE

— QUARTERLY REVIEW —

THIRD QUARTERLY REVIEW

Big accomplishments in the last 25 days:

1.

2.

3.

Areas I need to improve in the next 25 days:

1.

2.

3.

I am proud that:

I am excited about:

I am surprised by:

Thoughts/ideas/musings:

_____
_____
_____
_____
_____

CONGRATULATIONS!
YOU'VE COMPLETED 75% OF YOUR 100 DAYS!

DAY 76   Date:

We should be taught not to wait for inspiration to start a thing. Action always generates inspiration. Inspiration seldom generates action. —FRANK TIBOLT

I am grateful for:

In 24 days I will:

My #1 focus today is:

By the end of the day I will have accomplished these three measurable objectives that support my S.M.A.R.T. goal.

1.

2.

3.

Action plan for the day:

O

O

O

O

O

Thoughts/ideas/musings:

_____

_____

_____

_____

Recommended Resource: JoshShipp.com: Josh helps adults understand teens and teens understand themselves.

NIGHT 76

Two wonderful things that happened today:

1.

2.

Two struggles I encountered:

1.

2.

Possible solutions for these struggles:

1.

2.

Tomorrow will be a great day because:

_____

_____

_____

_____

_____

Final thought of the day:

_____

_____

_____

_____

_____

 Goodnight, Fire Nation!

DAY 77   Date:

It's not that I'm so smart, it's just that
I stay with problems longer. —ALBERT EINSTEIN

I am grateful for:

In 23 days I will:

My #1 focus today is:

By the end of the day I will have accomplished these three measurable objectives that support my S.M.A.R.T. goal.

1.

2.

3.

Action plan for the day:

O

O

O

O

O

Thoughts/ideas/musings:

_____

_____

_____

_____

Recommended Resource: PodcastWebsites.com: All-in-one peace of mind for podcasters. Website, media hosting and 24-7 support.

NIGHT 77

Two wonderful things that happened today:

1.

2.

Two struggles I encountered:

1.

2.

Possible solutions for these struggles:

1.

2.

Tomorrow will be a great day because:

_____

_____

_____

_____

_____

Final thought of the day:

_____

_____

_____

_____

_____

 Goodnight, Fire Nation!

DAY 78   Date:

Many of life's failures are people who did not realize how close they were to success when they gave up. —THOMAS EDISON

I am grateful for:

In 22 days I will:

My #1 focus today is:

By the end of the day I will have accomplished these three measurable objectives that support my S.M.A.R.T. goal.

1.

2.

3.

Action plan for the day:

O

O

O

O

O

Thoughts/ideas/musings:

_____

_____

_____

_____

Recommended Resource: ActiveInbox: Turn Gmail into a GTD task manager.

NIGHT 78

Two wonderful things that happened today:

1.

2.

Two struggles I encountered:

1.

2.

Possible solutions for these struggles:

1.

2.

Tomorrow will be a great day because:

_____

_____

_____

_____

_____

Final thought of the day:

_____

_____

_____

_____

_____

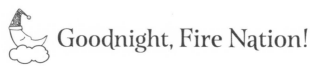 Goodnight, Fire Nation!

DAY 79 Date:

Ask yourself this question:
"Will this matter a year from now?" —RICHARD CARLSON

I am grateful for:

In 21 days I will:

My #1 focus today is:

By the end of the day I will have accomplished these three measurable objectives that support my S.M.A.R.T. goal.

1.

2.

3.

Action plan for the day:

○

○

○

○

○

Thoughts/ideas/musings:

_____

_____

_____

_____

Recommended Resource: Canva: A free tool that makes design simple for everyone. Create designs for web or print: blog graphics, presentations, Facebook covers, flyers, posters, invitations and more.

NIGHT 79

Two wonderful things that happened today:

1.

2.

Two struggles I encountered:

1.

2.

Possible solutions for these struggles:

1.

2.

Tomorrow will be a great day because:

_____

_____

_____

_____

_____

Final thought of the day:

_____

_____

_____

_____

_____

 Goodnight, Fire Nation!

DAY 80 Date:

As I look back on my life, I realize that every time I thought I was being rejected from something good, I was actually being redirected to something better. —DR. STEVE MARABOLI

I am grateful for:

In 20 days I will:

My #1 focus today is:

By the end of the day I will have accomplished these three measurable objectives that support my S.M.A.R.T. goal.

1.

2.

3.

Action plan for the day:

O

O

O

O

O

Thoughts/ideas/musings:

_____

_____

_____

_____

Recommended Resource: ChrisDucker.com: Chris shares how you can start, run and grow a business in the 21st century.

NIGHT 80

Two wonderful things that happened today:

1.

2.

Two struggles I encountered:

1.

2.

Possible solutions for these struggles:

1.

2.

Tomorrow will be a great day because:

_____
_____
_____
_____
_____

Final thought of the day:

_____
_____
_____
_____
_____

 Goodnight, Fire Nation!

You're 20 days away from accomplishing your #1 goal!

Finish strong and keep your momentum going strong by ordering your next Freedom Journal today at **TheFreedomJournal.com**

GAUGING YOUR PACE

—10-DAY SPRINT RECAP—

10-DAY SPRINT RECAP

My major accomplishment during this sprint:

_____

_____

_____

My two biggest struggles during this sprint:

1.

2.

Two possible solutions to these struggles:

1.

2.

_____

Sow an act and you reap a habit. Sow a habit and you reap a character. Sow a character and you reap a destiny. —CHARLES READE

_____

Thoughts/ideas/musings:

_____

_____

_____

_____

_____

Fill in your current progress to your 100-day goal!　　　⌐ BONUS ⌐

　　　25%　　　　50%　　　　75%　　　100%　　　125%

CONGRATULATIONS!
YOU'VE COMPLETED 80% OF YOUR 100 DAYS!

ON YOUR MARK

10-DAY SPRINT

NINTH 10-DAY SPRINT

The micro-goal I will accomplish during this sprint:

_____

_____

_____

Three specific actions I will take to accomplish this micro-goal:

1.

2.

3.

One habit I will implement over the next 10 days:

My action plan to implement this habit:

_____

_____

_____

It's time to IGNITE!

DAY 81   Date:

What if I told you that 10 years from now, your life would be exactly the same?
I doubt you'd be happy. So, why are you so afraid of change?

—KAREN SALMANSOHN

I am grateful for:

In 19 days I will:

My #1 focus today is:

By the end of the day I will have accomplished these three measurable objectives that support my S.M.A.R.T. goal.

1.

2.

3.

Action plan for the day:

○

○

○

○

○

Thoughts/ideas/musings:

_____

_____

_____

_____

Recommended Resource: Gratitude App: The #1 gratitude journal app for over five years. Use it for at least three weeks and your life will never be the same again.

NIGHT 81

Two wonderful things that happened today:

1.

2.

Two struggles I encountered:

1.

2.

Possible solutions for these struggles:

1.

2.

Tomorrow will be a great day because:

_____

_____

_____

_____

_____

Final thought of the day:

_____

_____

_____

_____

 Goodnight, Fire Nation!

DAY 82   Date:

Perseverance is the hard work you do after you get tired of doing the hard work you already did. —NEWT GINGRICH

I am grateful for:

In 18 days I will:

My #1 focus today is:

By the end of the day I will have accomplished these three measurable objectives that support my S.M.A.R.T. goal.

1.

2.

3.

Action plan for the day:

O

O

O

O

O

Thoughts/ideas/musings:

_____

_____

_____

_____

Recommended Resource: Zoom: This cloud meeting company unifies mobile collaboration, cloud video conferencing and simple online meetings into one easy-to-use platform.

NIGHT 82

Two wonderful things that happened today:

1.

2.

Two struggles I encountered:

1.

2.

Possible solutions for these struggles:

1.

2.

Tomorrow will be a great day because:

_____
_____
_____
_____
_____

Final thought of the day:

_____
_____
_____
_____

 Goodnight, Fire Nation!

DAY 83 Date:

We will either find a way or make one. —HANNIBAL

I am grateful for:

In 17 days I will:

My #1 focus today is:

By the end of the day I will have accomplished these three measurable objectives that support my S.M.A.R.T. goal.

1.

2.

3.

Action plan for the day:

O

O

O

O

O

Thoughts/ideas/musings:

_____

_____

_____

_____

Recommended Resource: AquaNotes: Waterproof paper notepad. Never let another great idea go down the drain.

NIGHT 83

Two wonderful things that happened today:

1.

2.

Two struggles I encountered:

1.

2.

Possible solutions for these struggles:

1.

2.

Tomorrow will be a great day because:

_____

_____

_____

_____

_____

Final thought of the day:

_____

_____

_____

_____

_____

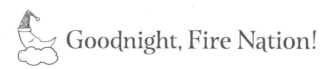 Goodnight, Fire Nation!

DAY 84   Date:

The best way out is always through. —ROBERT FROST

I am grateful for:

In 16 days I will:

My #1 focus today is:

By the end of the day I will have accomplished these three measurable objectives that support my S.M.A.R.T. goal.

1.

2.

3.

Action plan for the day:

O

O

O

O

O

Thoughts/ideas/musings:

_____

_____

_____

_____

Recommended Resource: MichaelHyatt.com: Michael discusses how to lead with purpose, personal productivity, book publishing, and social media.

NIGHT 84

Two wonderful things that happened today:

1.

2.

Two struggles I encountered:

1.

2.

Possible solutions for these struggles:

1.

2.

Tomorrow will be a great day because:

_____

_____

_____

_____

_____

Final thought of the day:

_____

_____

_____

_____

_____

 Goodnight, Fire Nation!

DAY 85   Date:

A winner is just a loser who tried one more time. —GEORGE M. MOORE JR.

I am grateful for:

In 15 days I will:

My #1 focus today is:

By the end of the day I will have accomplished these three measurable objectives that support my S.M.A.R.T. goal.

1.

2.

3.

Action plan for the day:

O

O

O

O

O

Thoughts/ideas/musings:

_____

_____

_____

_____

Recommended Resource: Airbnb: Discover amazing, unique accommodations in 190 countries. Airbnb is the world leader in travel rentals.

NIGHT 85

Two wonderful things that happened today:

1.

2.

Two struggles I encountered:

1.

2.

Possible solutions for these struggles:

1.

2.

Tomorrow will be a great day because:

_____

_____

_____

_____

_____

Final thought of the day:

_____

_____

_____

_____

_____

 Goodnight, Fire Nation!

DAY 86 Date:

Obsessed is a word that the lazy use
to describe the dedicated. —UNKNOWN

I am grateful for:

In 14 days I will:

My #1 focus today is:

By the end of the day I will have accomplished these three measurable objectives that support my S.M.A.R.T. goal.

1.

2.

3.

Action plan for the day:

O

O

O

O

O

Thoughts/ideas/musings:

_____

_____

_____

_____

Recommended Resource: MyFitnessPal: Over 50 million people have lost weight with MyFitnessPal's free calorie counter. Get free access to the world's largest nutrition and calorie database.

NIGHT 86

Two wonderful things that happened today:

1.

2.

Two struggles I encountered:

1.

2.

Possible solutions for these struggles:

1.

2.

Tomorrow will be a great day because:

_____
_____
_____
_____
_____

Final thought of the day:

_____
_____
_____
_____
_____

 Goodnight, Fire Nation!

DAY 87   Date:

Do more of what makes you happy. —CARMEL MCCONNELL

I am grateful for:

In 13 days I will:

My #1 focus today is:

By the end of the day I will have accomplished these three measurable objectives that support my S.M.A.R.T. goal.

1.

2.

3.

Action plan for the day:

○

○

○

○

○

Thoughts/ideas/musings:

_____

_____

_____

_____

Recommended Resource: LivePlan: Creating a business plan has never been easier. LivePlan Business Plan Software takes you through the process to create investor-ready business plans.

NIGHT 87

Two wonderful things that happened today:

1.

2.

Two struggles I encountered:

1.

2.

Possible solutions for these struggles:

1.

2.

Tomorrow will be a great day because:

_____

_____

_____

_____

_____

Final thought of the day:

_____

_____

_____

_____

_____

 Goodnight, Fire Nation!

DAY 88 Date:

Success is the ability to go from failure to failure without losing your enthusiasm. —WINSTON CHURCHILL

I am grateful for:

In 12 days I will:

My #1 focus today is:

By the end of the day I will have accomplished these three measurable objectives that support my S.M.A.R.T. goal.

1.

2.

3.

Action plan for the day:

○

○

○

○

○

Thoughts/ideas/musings:

_____

_____

_____

_____

Recommended Resource: 48Days.net: A networking site started by Dan Miller for people who want to generate their own income, full time or part time.

NIGHT 88

Two wonderful things that happened today:

1.

2.

Two struggles I encountered:

1.

2.

Possible solutions for these struggles:

1.

2.

Tomorrow will be a great day because:

_____

_____

_____

_____

_____

Final thought of the day:

_____

_____

_____

_____

_____

 Goodnight, Fire Nation!

DAY 89 Date:

Great things are done by a series of small things brought together. —VINCENT VAN GOGH

I am grateful for:

In 11 days I will:

My #1 focus today is:

By the end of the day I will have accomplished these three measurable objectives that support my S.M.A.R.T. goal.

1.

2.

3.

Action plan for the day:

○

○

○

○

○

Thoughts/ideas/musings:

_____

_____

_____

_____

Recommended Resource: Chimpadeedoo: Collects email addresses and stores them locally on your iPad or Android tablet, even when you're not online.

247

NIGHT 89

Two wonderful things that happened today:

1.

2.

Two struggles I encountered:

1.

2.

Possible solutions for these struggles:

1.

2.

Tomorrow will be a great day because:

_____

_____

_____

_____

_____

Final thought of the day:

_____

_____

_____

_____

 Goodnight, Fire Nation!

DAY 90 Date:

The man who moves a mountain begins
by carrying away small stones. —CONFUCIUS

I am grateful for:

In 10 days I will:

My #1 focus today is:

By the end of the day I will have accomplished these three measurable objectives that support my S.M.A.R.T. goal.

1.

2.

3.

Action plan for the day:

○

○

○

○

○

Thoughts/ideas/musings:

_____
_____
_____
_____

Recommended Resource: PayPal: The faster, safer way to send money, make an online payment, receive money or set up a merchant account.

NIGHT 90

Two wonderful things that happened today:

1.

2.

Two struggles I encountered:

1.

2.

Possible solutions for these struggles:

1.

2.

Tomorrow will be a great day because:

_____

_____

_____

_____

_____

Final thought of the day:

_____

_____

_____

_____

 Goodnight, Fire Nation!

GAUGING YOUR PACE

—10-DAY SPRINT RECAP—

10-DAY SPRINT RECAP

My major accomplishment during this sprint:

_____

_____

_____

My two biggest struggles during this sprint:

1.

2.

Two possible solutions to these struggles:

1.

2.

A nail is driven out by another nail. Habit is overcome by habit. —DESIDERIUS ERASMUS

Thoughts/ideas/musings:

_____

_____

_____

_____

_____

Fill in your current progress to your 100-day goal!   ⌐ BONUS ⌐

     25%   50%   75%   100%   125%

CONGRATULATIONS! YOU'VE COMPLETED 90% OF YOUR 100 DAYS!

ON YOUR MARK

—— 10-DAY SPRINT ——

FINAL 10-DAY SPRINT

The micro-goal I will accomplish during this sprint:

_____

_____

_____

Three specific actions I will take to accomplish this micro-goal:

1.

2.

3.

One habit I will implement over the next 10 days:

My action plan to implement this habit:

_____

_____

_____

DAY 91 Date:

Courage doesn't always roar. Sometimes courage is the quiet voice at the end of the day saying, "I will try again tomorrow." —MARY ANNE RADMACHER

I am grateful for:

In 9 days I will:

My #1 focus today is:

By the end of the day I will have accomplished these three measurable objectives that support my S.M.A.R.T. goal.

1.

2.

3.

Action plan for the day:

O

O

O

O

O

Thoughts/ideas/musings:

_____

_____

_____

_____

Recommended Resource: WeChat: Available for all kinds of platforms; enjoy group chat; supports voice, photo, video and text messages.

NIGHT 91

Two wonderful things that happened today:

1.

2.

Two struggles I encountered:

1.

2.

Possible solutions for these struggles:

1.

2.

Tomorrow will be a great day because:

_____
_____
_____
_____
_____

Final thought of the day:

_____
_____
_____
_____
_____

 Goodnight, Fire Nation!

DAY 92 Date:

Dreaming, after all, is a form of planning. —GLORIA STEINEM

I am grateful for:

In 8 days I will:

My #1 focus today is:

By the end of the day I will have accomplished these three measurable objectives that support my S.M.A.R.T. goal.

1.

2.

3.

Action plan for the day:

O

O

O

O

O

Thoughts/ideas/musings:

_____
_____
_____
_____

Recommended Resource: ContentMarketingInstitute.com: The essential content marketing education.

NIGHT 92

Two wonderful things that happened today:

1.

2.

Two struggles I encountered:

1.

2.

Possible solutions for these struggles:

1.

2.

Tomorrow will be a great day because:

_____

_____

_____

_____

_____

Final thought of the day:

_____

_____

_____

_____

_____

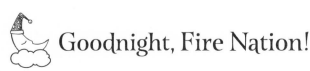 Goodnight, Fire Nation!

DAY 93 Date:

I am certain there is too much certainty in the world. —MICHAEL CRICHTON

I am grateful for:

In 7 days I will:

My #1 focus today is:

By the end of the day I will have accomplished these three measurable objectives that support my S.M.A.R.T. goal.

1.

2.

3.

Action plan for the day:

○

○

○

○

○

Thoughts/ideas/musings:

_____

_____

_____

_____

Recommended Resource: Haiku Deck: A completely new kind of presentation software—it's simple, beautiful, and fun.

NIGHT 93

Two wonderful things that happened today:

1.

2.

Two struggles I encountered:

1.

2.

Possible solutions for these struggles:

1.

2.

Tomorrow will be a great day because:

_____

_____

_____

_____

_____

Final thought of the day:

_____

_____

_____

_____

_____

 Goodnight, Fire Nation!

DAY 94 Date:

Go forth and set the world on fire. —ST. IGNATIUS

I am grateful for:

In 6 days I will:

My #1 focus today is:

By the end of the day I will have accomplished these three measurable objectives that support my S.M.A.R.T. goal.

1.

2.

3.

Action plan for the day:

O

O

O

O

O

Thoughts/ideas/musings:

_____

_____

_____

_____

Recommended Resource: Gumroad: Are you a creator? Start selling products directly to your audience today with Gumroad.

NIGHT 94

Two wonderful things that happened today:

1.

2.

Two struggles I encountered:

1.

2.

Possible solutions for these struggles:

1.

2.

Tomorrow will be a great day because:

_____
_____
_____
_____
_____

Final thought of the day:

_____
_____
_____
_____
_____

 Goodnight, Fire Nation!

DAY 95 Date:

I never could have done what I have done without the habits of punctuality, order, and diligence, without the determination to concentrate myself on one subject at a time. —CHARLES DICKENS

I am grateful for:

In 5 days I will:

My #1 focus today is:

By the end of the day I will have accomplished these three measurable objectives that support my S.M.A.R.T. goal.

1.

2.

3.

Action plan for the day:

O

O

O

O

O

Thoughts/ideas/musings:

_____

_____

_____

_____

Recommended Resource: theSkimm: The daily email newsletter that gives you everything you need to start your day. They do the reading for you—across subject lines and party lines.

NIGHT 95

Two wonderful things that happened today:

1.

2.

Two struggles I encountered:

1.

2.

Possible solutions for these struggles:

1.

2.

Tomorrow will be a great day because:

_____
_____
_____
_____
_____

Final thought of the day:

_____
_____
_____
_____
_____

 Goodnight, Fire Nation!

Live as if you were to die tomorrow.
Learn as if you were to live forever. —MAHATMA GANDHI

I am grateful for:

In 4 days I will:

My #1 focus today is:

By the end of the day I will have accomplished these three measurable objectives that support my S.M.A.R.T. goal.

1.

2.

3.

Action plan for the day:

O

O

O

O

O

Thoughts/ideas/musings:

_____

_____

_____

_____

Recommended Resource: GretchenRubin.com: Learn about Gretchen's experiments in the pursuit of happiness and good habits.

NIGHT 96

Two wonderful things that happened today:

1.

2.

Two struggles I encountered:

1.

2.

Possible solutions for these struggles:

1.

2.

Tomorrow will be a great day because:

_____

_____

_____

_____

_____

Final thought of the day:

_____

_____

_____

_____

_____

 Goodnight, Fire Nation!

DAY 97 Date:

Every great dream begins with a dreamer. Always remember, you have within you the strength, the patience, and the passion to reach for the stars to change the world. —HARRIET TUBMAN

I am grateful for:

In 3 days I will:

My #1 focus today is:

By the end of the day I will have accomplished these three measurable objectives that support my S.M.A.R.T. goal.

1.

2.

3.

Action plan for the day:

O

O

O

O

O

Thoughts/ideas/musings:

_____

_____

_____

_____

Recommended Resource: EasilyDo: A virtual personal assistant app that makes you more productive and connected. A productivity app with no to-do lists.

NIGHT 97

Two wonderful things that happened today:

1.

2.

Two struggles I encountered:

1.

2.

Possible solutions for these struggles:

1.

2.

Tomorrow will be a great day because:

_____
_____
_____
_____
_____

Final thought of the day:

_____
_____
_____
_____
_____

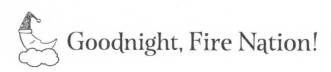 Goodnight, Fire Nation!

DAY 98   Date:

If you don't design your own life plan, chances are you'll fall into someone else's plan. And guess what they have planned for you? Not much. —JIM ROHN

I am grateful for:

In 2 days I will:

My #1 focus today is:

By the end of the day I will have accomplished these three measurable objectives that support my S.M.A.R.T. goal.

1.

2.

3.

Action plan for the day:

O

O

O

O

O

Thoughts/ideas/musings:

_____

_____

_____

_____

Recommended Resource: Streak: Connects securely to Google Apps. Use work, personal, and school Gmail accounts.

NIGHT 98

Two wonderful things that happened today:

1.

2.

Two struggles I encountered:

1.

2.

Possible solutions for these struggles:

1.

2.

Tomorrow will be a great day because:

_____

_____

_____

_____

_____

Final thought of the day:

_____

_____

_____

_____

_____

 Goodnight, Fire Nation!

DAY 99 Date:

If you want to make a permanent change, stop focusing on the size of your problems and start focusing on the size of you! —T. HARV EKER

I am grateful for:

In 1 day I will:

My #1 focus today is:

By the end of the day I will have accomplished these three measurable objectives that support my S.M.A.R.T. goal.

1.

2.

3.

Action plan for the day:

○

○

○

○

○

Thoughts/ideas/musings:

_____

_____

_____

_____

Recommended Resource: Wistia: Provides professional video hosting with amazing viewer analytics, HD video delivery, and marketing tools to help you understand your visitors.

NIGHT 99

Two wonderful things that happened today:

1.

2.

Two struggles I encountered:

1.

2.

Possible solutions for these struggles:

1.

2.

Tomorrow will be a great day because:

_____
_____
_____
_____
_____

Final thought of the day:

_____
_____
_____
_____
_____

 Goodnight, Fire Nation!

DAY 100   Date:

Repetition is the father of learning, I repeat, repetition is the father of learning. —DWAYNE MICHAEL CARTER

I am grateful for:

Today I will:

My #1 focus today is:

By the end of the day I will have accomplished these three measurable objectives that support my S.M.A.R.T. goal.

1.

2.

3.

Action plan for the day:

O

O

O

O

O

Thoughts/ideas/musings:

_____

_____

_____

_____

Recommended Resource: FreePodcastCourse.com: Learn how to create, grow, and monetize your podcast in 15 days, for free!

NIGHT 100

Two wonderful things that happened today:

1.

2.

Two struggles I encountered:

1.

2.

Possible solutions for these struggles:

1.

2.

Tomorrow will be a great day because:

_____

_____

_____

_____

_____

Final thought of the day:

_____

_____

_____

_____

 Goodnight, Fire Nation!

CONGRAT

ULATIONS!

CONGRATULATIONS!

A great accomplishment shouldn't be the end of the road, just the starting point for the next leap forward. —HARVEY MACKAY

You've been on quite the journey, and you should be incredibly proud of yourself.

I know this is just the beginning of many great things to come.

Take a deep breath and let it out slowly. Now revel in your success. You deserve it!

This feeling of accomplishment gets better as you continue to achieve your goals, so don't stop here!

Let's set your next S.M.A.R.T. goal right now, and if you haven't already, visit TheFreedomJournal.com to order your next Freedom Journal to keep up the HEAT!

IGNITE!

—John Lee Dumas

MY NEXT S.M.A.R.T. GOAL

It's time to set your NEXT goal!

In 100 days I will: _____

_____

_____

Specific

_____

_____

_____

Measurable

_____

_____

_____

Attainable

_____

_____

_____

Relevant

_____

_____

_____

Time-bound

_____

_____

_____

Are you ready to master
productivity, discipline, and focus in 100 days?

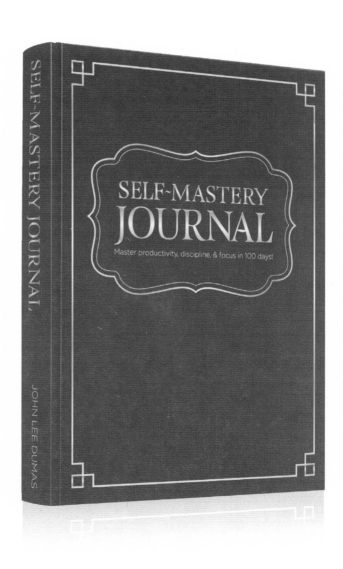

Then it's time for:

SELF~MASTERY
JOURNAL

Master productivity, discipline, & focus in 100 days!

By John Lee Dumas

THE resource that will guide
you in mastering your productivity,
discipline, and focus in 100 days.

Learn more at:

SelfMasteryJournal.com

CALENDAR

DATE:	DATE:	DATE:	DATE:	DATE:
10-DAY SPRINT				
DATE:	DATE:	DATE:	DATE:	DATE:
DATE:	DATE:	DATE:	DATE:	DATE:
10-DAY SPRINT				
DATE:	DATE:	DATE:	DATE:	DATE:
DATE:	DATE:	DATE:	DATE:	DATE:
10-DAY SPRINT				QUARTERLY REVIEW
DATE:	DATE:	DATE:	DATE:	DATE:
DATE:	DATE:	DATE:	DATE:	DATE:
10-DAY SPRINT				
DATE:	DATE:	DATE:	DATE:	DATE:
DATE:	DATE:	DATE:	DATE:	DATE:
10-DAY SPRINT				
DATE:	DATE:	DATE:	DATE:	DATE:
				QUARTERLY REVIEW

CALENDAR

DATE:	DATE:	DATE:	DATE:	DATE:
10-DAY SPRINT				
DATE:	DATE:	DATE:	DATE:	DATE:
DATE:	DATE:	DATE:	DATE:	DATE:
10-DAY SPRINT				
DATE:	DATE:	DATE:	DATE:	DATE:
DATE:	DATE:	DATE:	DATE:	DATE:
DATE:	DATE:	DATE:	DATE:	DATE:
10-DAY SPRINT				QUARTERLY REVIEW
DATE:	DATE:	DATE:	DATE:	DATE:
DATE:	DATE:	DATE:	DATE:	DATE:
10-DAY SPRINT				
DATE:	DATE:	DATE:	DATE:	DATE:
DATE:	DATE:	DATE:	DATE:	DATE:
10-DAY SPRINT				
DATE:	DATE:	DATE:	DATE:	DATE:

THOUGHTS/IDEAS/MUSINGS

THOUGHTS/IDEAS/MUSINGS

THOUGHTS/IDEAS/MUSINGS

THOUGHTS/IDEAS/MUSINGS

THOUGHTS/IDEAS/MUSINGS

THOUGHTS/IDEAS/MUSINGS

THOUGHTS/IDEAS/MUSINGS

THOUGHTS/IDEAS/MUSINGS

THOUGHTS/IDEAS/MUSINGS

THOUGHTS/IDEAS/MUSINGS

THOUGHTS/IDEAS/MUSINGS

THOUGHTS/IDEAS/MUSINGS

THOUGHTS/IDEAS/MUSINGS

THOUGHTS/IDEAS/MUSINGS

THOUGHTS/IDEAS/MUSINGS

THOUGHTS/IDEAS/MUSINGS

THOUGHTS/IDEAS/MUSINGS

THOUGHTS/IDEAS/MUSINGS

THOUGHTS/IDEAS/MUSINGS

THOUGHTS/IDEAS/MUSINGS

RESOURCES

DAY 1 Hootsuite: Enhance your social media management with Hootsuite, the leading social media dashboard.

DAY 2 WorkFlowy: An organizational tool that makes life easier. It's a surprisingly powerful way to take notes, make lists, collaborate, brainstorm, and plan.

DAY 3 Buffer: Makes it easy to share any page you're reading. Keep your Buffer topped up and they automatically share posts for you throughout the day.

DAY 4 FourHourWorkWeek.com: #1 *New York Times* best-selling author Tim Ferriss teaches you how to escape the 9-5, live anywhere, and join the new rich.

DAY 5 Lynda: Learn software, creative, and business skills to achieve your personal and professional goals.

DAY 6 Fiverr: The place for people to share things they're willing to do for $5.

DAY 7 Evernote: The Evernote family of products help you remember and act upon ideas, projects and experiences across all the computers, phones and tablets you use.

DAY 8 EOFire.com: In his award-winning podcast, John Lee Dumas chats with today's most inspiring entrepreneurs 7 days a week. Prepare to IGNITE!

DAY 9 Jing: Try Jing for a free and simple way to start sharing images and short videos of your computer screen. For work, home, or play.

DAY 10 Asana: Teamwork without email. Asana puts conversations and tasks together, so you can get more done with less effort.

DAY 11 Dropbox: Dropbox is a free service that lets you bring your photos, docs, and videos anywhere and share them easily. Never email yourself a file again!

DAY 12 MarcandAngel.com: Marc and Angel share practical tips and ideas on life, hacks, productivity, aspirations, health, work, tech and general self-improvement.

RESOURCES

DAY 13 TaskRabbit: Get just about anything done by friendly, trustworthy people. Vetted TaskRabbits can help with errands, cleaning, delivery and so much more.

DAY 14 Coach.me: Coach.me employs coaching, community, and data to help you be your best. Stay motivated with guidance and encouragement.

DAY 15 Trello: Infinitely flexible. Incredibly easy to use. Great mobile apps. It's free. Trello keeps track of everything, from the big picture to the minute details.

DAY 16 ChrisBrogan.com: Chris Brogan is an American author, journalist, marketing consultant, and speaker about social media marketing.

DAY 17 Rapportive: Rapportive shows you everything about your contacts right inside your inbox. They combine what you know, what your organization knows, and what the web contains.

DAY 18 Vocaroo: Vocaroo is a quick and easy way to share voice messages over the internet.

DAY 19 RescueTime: Helps you understand your daily habits so you can focus and be more productive.

DAY 20 AmyPorterfield.com: Amy Porterfield is a social media strategy consultant.

DAY 21 Anti-Social: You know when you're trying to get work done, but end up wasting time on Facebook and Twitter? Anti-Social solves that problem.

DAY 22 TimeTrade: Online appointment scheduling by TimeTrade is used by businesses to create new sales prospects, accelerate the sales and service process, and make it easy.

DAY 23 Wunderlist: The easiest way to organize your life and business, whether you're planning an overseas adventure or sharing a shopping list with a loved one.

DAY 24 The SmartPassiveIncome Blog: Learn how to build an online passive income business with Pat Flynn.

RESOURCES

DAY 25 LeadPages: The world's easiest landing page generator. It's the easiest way to build conversion optimized and mobile responsive landing pages.

DAY 26 ScreenFlow: With ScreenFlow you can record the contents of your entire monitor while also capturing your video camera, iOS device, microphone and your computer audio.

DAY 27 Visual Website Optimizer: The world's easiest A/B testing tool.

DAY 28 HowToFascinate.com: Sally Hogshead is a world-class branding expert and best-selling author.

DAY 29 MindMeister: Create, share and collaboratively work on mind maps with MindMeister, the leading online mind mapping software. Includes apps for iPhone, iPad and Android.

DAY 30 TextExpander: Type more with less effort. TextExpander saves you time and keystrokes, expanding custom keyboard shortcuts into frequently used text and pictures.

DAY 31 Optimizely: Improve conversions through A/B testing, split testing and multivariate testing.

DAY 32 ViewFromTheTop.com: Aaron Walker is a business and life coach.

DAY 33 PicMonkey: Edit photos, create collages, add text and more. Get PicMonkey Royale for ads-free editing plus access to primo effects.

DAY 34 Unroll.Me: Toss the junk with one click. After you sign up, see a list of all your subscription emails. Unsubscribe instantly from whatever you don't want.

DAY 35 Virtual Staff Finder: A one-stop hub for hiring a virtual assistant.

DAY 36 HalElrod.com: Hal Elrod is a #1 best-selling author of *The Miracle Morning*.

DAY 37 Sleep Cycle: Using the accelerometer in your phone to monitor your movement during different sleep phases, Sleep Cycle tracks your sleep patterns and wakes you during your lightest sleep phase.

RESOURCES

DAY 38 KeePass: This free open source password manager helps you manage your passwords securely.

DAY 39 Zapier: Unlock the hidden power of your apps. Zapier connects the web apps you use to easily move your data and automate tedious tasks.

DAY 40 BoostBlogTraffic: Jon Morrow shares how to get more readers, become an authority in your niche, and get the attention you deserve.

DAY 41 Skitch: Get your point across with fewer words using annotation, shapes and sketches, so that your ideas become reality faster.

DAY 42 ScheduleOnce: A sophisticated online scheduling platform that works in tandem with Google Calendar and supports your business in a wide range of scheduling scenarios.

DAY 43 Contactually: This web-based CRM tool will help maximize your network ROI.

DAY 44 Ziglar.com: Ziglar strives to be the difference-maker in people's personal, family and professional success.

DAY 45 IFTTT: Put the internet to work for you.

DAY 46 Post Planner: Free up 2 hours daily with Post Planner's powerhouse Post Scheduler for Facebook. Never run out of Like-worthy posts.

DAY 47 Clarity.fm: Get on-demand business advice from experts, and make faster and better decisions to grow your business.

DAY 48 JonathanFields.com: Jonathan is on a quest to create and curate ideas, stories and tools that'll help you come alive.

DAY 49 Feedly: All your favorite websites in one place. Instead of having to hunt down news, Feedly aggregates and delivers the content of your favorite sites.

DAY 50 SelfControl: A free and open-source application for Mac OS X (10.5 or above) that lets you block your own access to distracting websites, your mail servers, etc.

RESOURCES

DAY 51 Pocket: Save for later. Put articles, videos or pretty much anything into Pocket. Save directly from your browser or from apps like Twitter, Flipboard, Pulse and Zite.

DAY 52 LewisHowes.com: Lewis will show you how to do what you love full time.

DAY 53 Mint: Does all the work of organizing and categorizing your spending for you. See where every dime goes.

DAY 54 TripIt: This travel organizing app keeps all of your travel plans in one spot. Create a master itinerary, and access your travel plans on any device.

DAY 55 AudioBooks: Download audiobooks online. Visit EOFireBook.com for a free audiobook today!

DAY 56 SimpleGreenSmoothies.com: This website is full of green smoothie recipes so you can transform your body from the inside out.

DAY 57 SaneBox: SaneBox intelligently analyzes your emails and filters your inbox of spam and unimportant messages.

DAY 58 DocuSign: Securely sign and manage documents online from any device with the most widely used e-signature solution.

DAY 59 Upwork: Find freelancers and freelance jobs on Upwork, the world's largest online workplace, where savvy businesses and professional freelancers go to work.

DAY 60 LiveYourLegend.net: Scott Dinsmore shares how to change the world by doing work you love.

DAY 61 Meetup.com: Helps groups of people with shared interests plan events and facilitates offline group meetings in various localities around the world.

DAY 62 Headspace: A course of guided meditation, delivered via an app or online. Try Headspace's starter course, Take10, for free today.

DAY 63 OmmWriter: A simple text processor that's all about making writing pleasurable again.

RESOURCES

DAY 64 Fizzle.co: Training from experts you trust and access to a virtual community of like-minded entrepreneurs.

DAY 65 Lucidchart: A visual collaboration tool that makes diagramming fast and easy.

DAY 66 Meet Edgar: The only app that stops social media updates from going to waste.

DAY 67 Fancy Hands: A team of assistants ready to work for you now. For a low monthly membership fee, you'll finally get the help you need.

DAY 68 SuperHumanEntrepreneur.com: Dr. Issac Jones guides the minds and spirits of entrepreneurs.

DAY 69 iDoneThis: An incredible management tool that provides unprecedented visibility into your productivity and areas for improvement.

DAY 70 Zirtual: A virtual executive assistant service that matches busy people with dedicated personal assistants.

DAY 71 Sprout Social: A social media management tool created to help businesses find new customers and grow their social media presence.

DAY 72 TheShawnStevensonModel.com: Shawn's mission is to help you become the strongest, healthiest, happiest version of yourself.

DAY 73 TeuxDeux: A bare-bones, but visually compelling and highly usable to-do app.

DAY 74 Boomerang: Adds scheduled sending and the easiest, most integrated email reminders to Gmail, helping you reach Inbox Zero.

DAY 75 Eventbrite: Brings people together through live experiences. Discover events that match your passions, or create your own with online ticketing tools.

DAY 76 JoshShipp.com: Josh helps adults understand teens and teens understand themselves.

RESOURCES

DAY 77 PodcastWebsites.com: All-in-one peace of mind for podcasters. Website, media hosting and 24-7 support.

DAY 78 ActiveInbox: Turn Gmail into a GTD task manager.

DAY 79 Canva: A free tool that makes design simple for everyone. Create designs for web or print: blog graphics, presentations, Facebook covers, flyers, posters, invitations and more.

DAY 80 ChrisDucker.com: Chris shares how you can start, run and grow a business in the 21st century.

DAY 81 Gratitude App: The #1 gratitude journal app for over five years. Use it for at least three weeks and your life will never be the same again.

DAY 82 Zoom: This cloud meeting company unifies mobile collaboration, cloud video conferencing and simple online meetings into one easy-to-use platform.

DAY 83 AquaNotes: Waterproof paper notepad. Never let another great idea go down the drain.

DAY 84 MichaelHyatt.com: Michael discusses how to lead with purpose, personal productivity, book publishing, and social media.

DAY 85 Airbnb: Discover amazing, unique accommodations in 190 countries. Airbnb is the world leader in travel rentals.

DAY 86 MyFitnessPal: Over 50 million people have lost weight with MyFitnessPal's free calorie counter. Get free access to the world's largest nutrition and calorie database.

DAY 87 LivePlan: Creating a business plan has never been easier. LivePlan Business Plan Software takes you through the process to create investor-ready business plans.

DAY 88 48Days.net: A networking site started by Dan Miller for people who want to generate their own income, full time or part time.

DAY 89 Chimpadeedoo: Collects email addresses and stores them locally on your iPad or Android tablet, even when you're not online.

RESOURCES

DAY 90 PayPal: The faster, safer way to send money, make an online payment, receive money or set up a merchant account.

DAY 91 WeChat: Available for all kinds of platforms; enjoy group chat; supports voice, photo, video and text messages.

DAY 92 ContentMarketingInstitute.com: The essential content marketing education.

DAY 93 Haiku Deck: A completely new kind of presentation software—it's simple, beautiful, and fun.

DAY 94 Gumroad: Are you a creator? Start selling products directly to your audience today with Gumroad.

DAY 95 theSkimm: The daily email newsletter that gives you everything you need to start your day. They do the reading for you—across subject lines and party lines.

DAY 96 GretchenRubin.com: Learn about Gretchen's experiments in the pursuit of happiness and good habits.

DAY 97 EasilyDo: A virtual personal assistant app that makes you more productive and connected. A productivity app with no to-do lists.

DAY 98 Streak: Connects securely to Google Apps. Use work, personal, and school Gmail accounts.

DAY 99 Wistia: Provides professional video hosting with amazing viewer analytics, HD video delivery, and marketing tools to help you understand your visitors.

DAY 100 FreePodcastCourse.com: Learn how to create, grow, and monetize your podcast in 15 days, for free!